Motor Vehicle Workshop Organization and Administration

BY

BERNARD CHANDLER

Chesterfield College of Technology

OXFORD UNIVERSITY PRESS

1972

Oxford University Press, Ely House, London W. 1

GLASGOW NEW YORK TORONTO MELBOURNE WELLINGTON
CAPE TOWN IBADAN NAIROBI DAR ES SALAAM LUSAKA ADDIS ABABA
DELHI BOMBAY CALCUTTA MADRAS KARACHI LAHORE DACCA
KUALA LUMPUR SINGAPORE HONG KONG TOKYO

A/658. 92

Printed in Great Britain
by J.W. Arrowsmith Ltd., Bristol

PREFACE

Modern garage operation requires considerable knowledge and skill. The days when a garage could be managed with little or no management knowledge are over.

To be an efficient manager of any motor vehicle workshop or service station, a man must have a good practical motor vehicle servicing background, an adequate knowledge of management practice, and a working knowledge of the law affecting the motor vehicle retail and repair trade. A manager's practical experience will come through his training as a motor vehicle mechanic or technician. His training for management must come through the careful study of techniques suited to his needs.

This book has been prepared to meet the requirements of existing managers wishing to extend their knowledge, prospective managers and trainees, as well as mechanics, receptionists, and others interested in the general operational requirements of service stations and workshops. To students taking the Full Technological Certificate of the City and Guilds of London Institute, the M.A.A./I.M.I. Diploma, and the Institute of Motor Industry Final examinations, this book will prove to be a very useful aid as it follows closely the syllabuses covering all matters for the examinations of these bodies.

I am very grateful to all members of the trade, trade organizations, manufacturers, training schools, and all others who have supplied the information so necessary for a book of this kind.

Metric sizes converted to English in the text are not necessarily precise conversion.

C.G.L.I. course numbers in the text are those allocated by the Institute in 1972. For the courses mentioned Appendix II details old and new C.G.L.I. numbers.

CONTENTS

ACKNOWLEDGEMENTS

The author would like to thank the organizations listed below for permission to publish the illustrations mentioned.

C. H. Allen Ltd.	Fig. 4.1
British Leyland Motor Corporation	Figs 2.1, 2.2, 2.13
Chrysler Motor Corporation	Figs 2.6, 2.7, 2.12
Garage Equipment Association	Fig. 1.3
Jessups Ltd.	Fig. 2.5
Kalamazoo Ltd.	Figs 2.3, 6.1
R.T.I.T.B.	Figs 5.3, 5.6
University Motors Ltd.	Fig. 2.8
Vauxhall Motor Co.	Figs 1.10, 2.4, 2.12, 2.14, 5.5

CHAPTER 1

LAYOUT

Layout of a service station

The layout of a service station in its entirety is a crucial factor in its profitability. No matter how efficient management and staff may be, no one will induce a customer to buy petrol from a service station which has difficult access points. Narrow entrances and badly placed petrol pumps mean time spent shunting a car in and out with the possibility of scratching it and, consequently, potential customers are lost. This however is only one aspect of service station layout. Reception area, accessories sales, workshop area, offices, toilets, and parts department all form part of the layout.

The site of the service station plays a very important part in its success. Very many factors have to be considered when an entirely new garage is being planned. Above everything is the obtaining of planning permission from the local council. Then there is traffic flow, existing competition, access points (that is whether entry is from one road or the service station is on a corner site, on cross roads with access from two roads), floating population either into or out of the area, and subsidies from oil and petrol companies for certain sites, to mention a few important aspects of site selection. Certain sites should be avoided; for example, sites where the population is dwindling, steep hills where it is dangerous and difficult to turn into a service station, one way street areas where access is obtainable from one side only, and similar situations are all poor and possibly disastrous choices. However, given a suitably accessible site with adequate car population the layout of the site must include the items listed.

Any progressive service station must consider new developments in garage repair and service work. The innovations of low-line servicing and diagnostic centres as aids to speedy and efficient work now form part of many service stations. A standard service station layout using a triangular site is shown in Fig. 1.1 and a variation to include a flow-line installation in Fig. 1.2

In both cases large parking areas are shown. From these areas cars are taken to the workshop area for major repair work or into the flow-line or fast service bay for servicing.

The reception area is clearly indicated by large clear signs, as are all areas including parking, toilets, and accessories, so that a customer can easily see where he wishes to go: this suggests efficiency. Customers like clear-cut signs without any confusion. Reception areas should be clean at all times and provide adequate seating where customers can wait, along with such amenities as tea-vending machines, magazines, and, very importantly, the accessories shop close by.

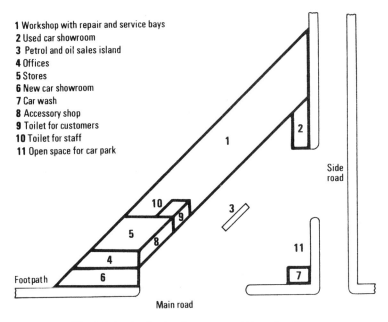

1 Workshop with repair and service bays
2 Used car showroom
3 Petrol and oil sales island
4 Offices
5 Stores
6 New car showroom
7 Car wash
8 Accessory shop
9 Toilet for customers
10 Toilet for staff
11 Open space for car park

.Fig. 1.1 Service Station Layout on a Triangular Site

Offices should be sited as shown so that accounting, invoicing, and other work can be efficiently executed with minimum delay to the customer. A suggested site layout by the Garage and Equipment Association is shown in Fig. 1.3. This needs little explanation and is a layout suitable for most types of service station work. The Motor Agents Association have grades of service stations which determine the type of work a service station will do, and most service stations are registered with the M.A.A. under a particular heading. For the different grades the following items are covered: workshop area available, equipment available (which includes lifts, ramps, and tools), towing facilities, stores-stocks held, staff—which includes recognized skilled staff (see Chapter 5), managerial staff with a minimum amount of experience (5 years for workshop, 2 years for the commercial side), wages and staff conditions of service, office accomodation and accounts and a 'sign' to indicate work undertaken. As these factors vary so does the type of membership available to the service station. Obviously some service stations offer very limited facilities such as

petrol sales and light repairs whilst others will offer complete services to include
all aspects of motor engineering work. Details of M.A.A. membership can be
obtained from the Secretary, Motor Agents Association, 201 Great Portland
Street, London, W.1. We can now consider each section of the Service Station
in detail.

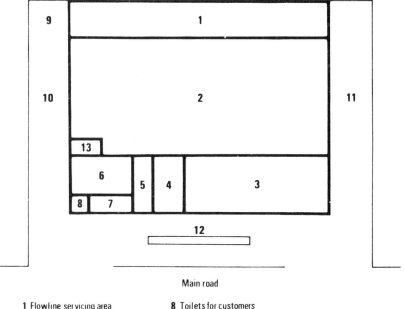

Main road

1 Flowline servicing area	8 Toilets for customers
2 Workshop area with repair bays	9 Open car park for flowline
3 Car showroom	10 Open car park for cars awaiting repairs
4 Stores	11 Open car park for cars awaiting collection by customers
5 Accessory shop	12 Petrol and oil sales island
6 Offices	13 Toilets and rest room for staff
7 Reception	

Fig. 1.2 Service Station Layout with a Flow-Line

Workshop layouts

The layout of any workshop will depend entirely upon the work anticipated
or work already being completed in the case of an existing service station.
Small workshops usually have a bench at the closed end of a workshop with
one pit or lift to enable work to be carried out underneath a car. In this modern age small workshops have a very limited value as modern vehicles demand
sophisticated equipment both to rapidly diagnose faults and as a means of
quality control following repair. To ensure a profitable workshop, floor space
must be used to the utmost. To emphasize this point let us assume floor
rental is £5 per square metre (1.2 square yards), per year. If an average car

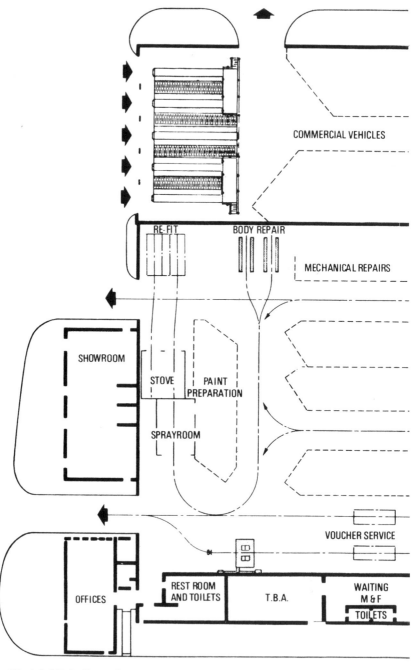

Fig. 1.3 G.E.A. Garage Layout

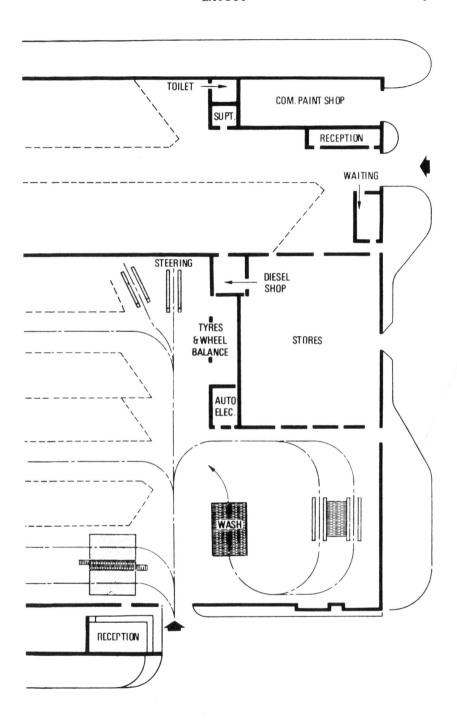

occupies a floor space of 10 square metres (11.9 square yards) during repair we can calculate the cost of a car occupying floor space for any length of time. Assuming the garage works 50 weeks with a 5 day week, the cost per day of 8 hours would be

$$\frac{£5 \times 10 \times 100 \text{ (pence)}}{50 \times 5 \times 8}$$

$$= 2\tfrac{1}{2}\text{p per hour.}$$

Floor rental space can be four times this amount in expensive areas, thus a car standing in a space and not being worked on could be costing 10p per hour or £0.8 for each working day for floor rental costs alone. A rough estimate therefore would be floor rental cost of £1 per day for an average car with floor rental costs at £20 per square metre per year (1.25 square yards).

The need to keep cars moving and for rapid completion of repairs and servicing is obvious. Apart from this, customers usually require a car as quickly as possible as a car off the road means loss earnings to them. So we have seen some major changes in service work to meet these demands. Flow-line servicing and diagnostic centres are but two innovations which we shall discuss in detail later. In the meantime, they must form part of large workshop layouts.

With a large workshop we can consider an area of, say, 50 metres (160 feet) by 30 metres (100 feet), that is 150 square metres (16 000 square feet). Utilization of an area of this size is shown in Fig. 1.4. Workshop areas with painted lines on a slope of 60° make it easy to run in and back out. Benches with steel tops and a 150 mm (6 in) jaw vice for every bay constitute basic equipment for repair work of a general nature. Jobs requiring use of a lift will move into the work area where lifts are part of standard equipment in the repair bays. At this point it should be stressed that wheel-free lifts are to be preferred and pits are to be avoided. Many serious accidents have occurred with pits when fumes have accumulated and caused serious poisoning. Other accidents have occurred when petrol has spilled into pits and gone unnoticed until a naked flame eventually ignited the vapour with terrible results for mechanics working underneath vehicles. Where pits are used they should be as wide as possible and have very easy access and exit points at frequent intervals.

With each repair bay there must be certain services. A power plug with 13 amp fuse, an air line connection, an inter communications connection at the bench for speaking direct to the stores for spare parts. This latter item enables a mechanic to order parts and have them brought to him without moving from the car; thus speeding up a repair job and saving the mechanics valuable time. A low powered, 24 volt, socket is also needed for pressurized safety inspection lamps. Alternatively, a bare overhead wire system with movable leads can be used as an inspection lighting method.

The bench itself should preferably be of steel with a steel vice of 150 mm (6 in) jaw as previously mentioned. A good size drawer capable of holding tools belonging to a mechanic should form part of the bench which should also have a second drawer or underspace to hold units whilst undergoing

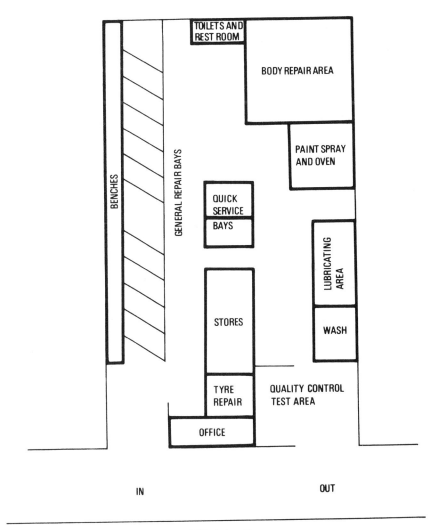

Fig. 1.4 Workshop Layout

repair, for example gearbox housings or cylinder blocks. Ideally, each bay should have means of lubrication but as there are many grades of oil a special bay is usually allocated for this purpose. Portable cranes of 1 000 kg to 2 000 kg (2 000 lb to 4 000 lb) capacity or overhead hoists on beams are also needed for lifting out engines and other heavy components.

Hydraulic trolley jacks of 2 tonne capacity along with stands also of suitable capacity should be readily accessible to each bay. Jacks, stands, wheel braces, wheel pullers, special extractors, stocks and dies should be kept in a central position in the stores so that a mechanic can use them and replace them immediately after use. A detailed list of tools which every major service station should have is given at the end of this chapter.

A four post lift which enables a car to be lifted and also allow a car to be lifted with its wheels free, is the best for all working conditions. There are a number of suppliers of these wheel-free lifts which enable inspections and repair of wheel hubs, brakes and drives to be worked on quite easily: the lubrication bay certainly needs such a lift. A mechanic's recommended tool list is given at the end of this chapter, to complete the requirements of a repair bay layout. Thus we have for general repair work a good working area for each bay of 6 metres (20 feet) by 3 metres (10 feet) to work around a car, good lighting, bench, vice, access to special tools, plug points, inspection lamp point, intercommunication system to stores, air line point and other special items which may be necessary for working on certain types of cars or commercial vehicles.

The servicing area

Now we must consider the type of servicing we are going to do. Is it to be (a) a single-speed bay servicing or (b) flow-line servicing? Also to be considered (a) cars (b) commercial vehicles. Both cars, and, especially, commercial vehicles will be longer, heavier and possibly wider in the future and due allowance must be made for these factors when planning any service area either on a single-speed bay or on a flow-line principle. It would be useless, for example, to plan a bay to service commercial vehicles on the present restricted length and tonnage.

Before we proceed to describe a flow-line system of servicing in detail let us consider the merits of the single bay and the idea behind flow-line servicing.

Flow-line servicing. This may be defined as the application of time and motion study to the servicing of cars and commercial vehicles. It can be seen to be derived from manufacturing methods on production lines. Similar terms which apply to production lines can also be usefully employed in garage workshops. Such terms are:

Job production. The completion of one particular type of job only, that is a 'one off' job. This is done occasionally in motor repair shops but usually repeat jobs are the case.

Batch production. This is the repeating of a few types of jobs of a similar pattern or nature. In production work repeat of identical jobs of small numbers comes under the heading of batch production.

Flow-line production. This is the continuous repeating of the same job, on production lines of several hundreds or thousands of the same kind of job. Applied to repair shops flow-line servicing does result in a continuous repeat of certain types of servicing work.

We must consider whether it is worth setting up a flow-line or not. Some manufacturers maintain it is not a practicable proposition and recommend the use of a well laid out service bay as being just as good or even better. On the other hand very good use of flow-lines has already been made to both garage, customer and mechanic. For example, some service stations have operated excellent flow-lines since 1966 and these will be referred to again later. One line can service 40 cars per day with 8 personnel but before we say this is not very impressive, the service given at this particular station far exceeds normal servicing requirements for very little extra cost.

Before a flow-line is considered, the volume of cars or commercial vehicles must merit the use of space and capital investment involved with equipment needed on the line. How can this be assessed? An obvious place not to put a flow-line is in a rural or country area where traffic is light. On the other hand a heavily congested area, such as any major city or large town, provides a sbource of supply of cars or commercial vehicles to feed a flow-line. Feeding the lines has proved a problem on occasions but overall they have been very successful. Further consideration must be the type of vehicle to go on the line. It is highly desirable to keep to one type of vehicle thus obtaining a constant supply of similar vehicles for example Ford Cortina or B.L.M.C. 1100. A little research into any area will reveal the popular type of car in the district. How many cars are needed to keep a line fully operational? If we say 25 cars a day on average making 125 per week, then for a 50 week year this will mean 7 250 cars of the same type in a particular district.

This number of course is with one service per year. As leisure time increases at least 2 services per year will be required by each car, thus reducing the number of cars to 3 625. Furthermore, it is not unlikely that all cars will eventually require an inspection and test certificate *every 6 months* or 12 000 miles whichever comes first. Bearing it in mind that lifting tackle and similar equipment which can involve danger to life and limb have been inspected and reports filed every 6 months for many years, is it unreasonable for the fast modern car and heavy commercial vehicle to be inspected and a report filed? Whilst not at present a practical proposition because of lack of D.O.E. facilities, it could eventually become a feature of future motor transport. Flow-lines are already used very successfully for pre D.O.E. Testing of Commercial Vehicles. Inspection at D.O.E. Testing Stations is also completed on a flow-line system. Cars and commercial vehicles can use such lines for checking new vehicles for pre-delivery checks. Manufacturers do rely on dealers to complete pre-delivery inspections and flow-line systems are ideal for this purpose.

Where other garages already offer a flow-line service close by, a reorganization would have to be considered, if customers are to be retained. The innovation of such lines in a district heavily populated with cars is certain to draw customers and, as will be seen when we inspect an actual service sheet, it also leads to more work in the workshop by detecting worn or dangerous parts when servicing and inspection is taking place. This repair work inevitably goes to the workshop where the flow-line is operating. It is quite possible to offer a service for all makes of cars on a flow-line basis but this can lead to problems as a flow-line must be operated on a time and motion study basis. Changing an oil filter on one car can take 3 minutes and on another 10 minutes, even longer on commercial vehicles. Thus it would be possible to create a blockage on a flow-line but once again we shall refer to this possibility later.

Perhaps a problem associated with flow-lines is the manning of the various stages. Men can get bored on one type of job and can lose interest in the work involved. For example a man constantly employed on one job, say checking an adjusting tappets, tightening cylinder head bolts and similar associated jobs on one stage of a flow-line, is bound to become bored and this can result in careless work. Production lines in car factories can suffer in a similar way. The way to overcome this is to have men on each stage 2 weeks at a time. If 6 stages are involved then 12 weeks on the line will be required before a man reverts back to stage 1. Some flow-line operators allow men to go back into a workshop after 4 or 5 weeks on the line. All men in the workshop take a turn on the flow-line. It is true to say, however, that some mechanics once having worked on flow-line servicing prefer to stay on the line rather than go back into a workshop on general repair work. Now if we look at the single bay system of servicing and compare this with a flow-line we can assess its merits. We have already seen that single bay operation is bound to operate when car population density does not merit flow-line operation. In areas where car density is heavy a single bay will, when operated efficiently, produce very good results. Some garages employ two mechanics in the bay to speed up service. Whilst one mechanic works on one part of the car the other works on another part. Where possible more than 2 mechanics can be employed but a stage is reached when too many mechanics can get in one anothers way. However, the judicious use of mechanics ina single bay can reduce considerably service time schedules set up by manufacturers. However, full flow-line operation usually includes many more items than those included on normal service and a customer gets very good value for money. A single service bay cannot usually employ all the equipment necessary for some services and cars have got to be shunted from the single bay to another area for a brake test, chassis dynamometer test or other specialized part of a service check. Single bay servicing has been in use for many years, almost since the invention of the motor car and has been successful. It still is successful but the future of service work is bound either to make service bays fully comprehensive for all equipment or lead to the adoption of a flow-line system. A speed bay fully equipped means one bay occupied with one or two mechanics working on a car. On a flow-line the equipment is distributed along the line with mechanics at each stage: a continuous flow of cars move along the line and this system must result in greater productivity. Cars in a single bay have to be driven in and out. If the bay is against a wall the car has to be backed out following a service and shunted about with loss of time as the car is handled. Each car has to be handled this way. Some workshops now employ a drive-in–drive-out service bay saving time by having good access and exit points and approaching the idea of a flow-line.

So we have now assessed the objects and ideas of single bay and flow-line servicing. Only the garage owner can decide if a flow-line will pay. In a heavily populated area any service station owner would do well to dwell on what has been written. Furthermore since the end of the 1939–1945 war the car population has steadily increased, almost doubling every 10 years. In 1969 10 million cars were registered, by 1980, 18 million cars are expected to be on the roads in Britain. The Electrical Development Association along with motor manufacturers, estimate that 20% of the 18 million are expected to be all-electric driven cars. Who can say in this fast changing but constantly expanding industry what we can expect by the year 1990 or 2 000. Progressive garage owners must be prepared to meet the present and future demands of the car servicing industry and one of the ways to meet these demands is either by installing a flow-line or by reorganizing existing premises and equipment to operate on a flow-line system. Many service stations have installed equipment on a piecemeal basis over the years to meet immediate needs and consequently have equipment located in various parts of a workshop which really needs to be re-organized to obtain a much better return for the owner.

Let us assume then that a flow-line is to be considered. Here is the procedure to be adopted.

Planning a flow-line

As motor manufacturers issue service requirements for all vehicles the implementation of the work on a flow-line basis should be considered as follows:
1) Decide and list the problems to be solved. Include the following items:
   a) All the jobs requiring attention, i.e. oil changes and/or checks, tappet adjustments, contact breaker point adjustment, etc.
   b) Location of each of these jobs on the flow-line.
   c) The time required to execute each job: where not given by the manufacturer a stop-watch check should be made to obtain an average time.
   d) The staff required for each job so that a smooth flow can be obtained and bottle-necks avoided. For example, if 6 stages of 10 minutes are envisaged then work for 10 minutes in each stage must be carefully allocated. Car inspection and lubrication can cause congestion and duplication of this section is sometimes required, for example two lifts or pits. Such duplication allows a car on a minor service to bypass one on a larger service.

2) Assess the benefits to be gained for having a flow-line in your workshops i.e. skilled, semi-skilled and unskilled workers placed at correct places with minimum waste of time. Also, equipment placed in a logical order to obtain maximum use and profitability from it can be considered.

3) Calculate the *area* to be required for such a service, the *capital expenditure* needed for equipment or removal of existing equipment, *overheads* involved for rental, services etc., and the *total staff* required, so arriving at the cost.

4) The *revenue* which can be expected from the service should then be calculated. Operational expenses and depreciation of equipment should be deducted from the revenue, to calculte the total net *profit*.

5) When all calculations are complete and it is certain that a profit will be made and increased over previous servicing methods then installation of the line can proceed. Much useful advice and financial aid can be obtained from oil companies who have experience in this field. Personnel in charge of such work at the oil companies are usually referred to as 'Dealer Planning Engineers'. These are the people to be contacted for all practical advice and any servicing or workshop manager would be wise to seek their advice.

Ideas for flow-line layouts

It is now necessary to see how a flow-line is arranged. We have considered the basic requirements and now the layouts themselves need some study. Ideally, a flow-line on a continuous straight line is best with sufficient width to enable a vehicle to be shunted off the line if necessary. Consider the service offered, layout and personnel required for a standard basic car of all makes bearing in mind some of the pitfalls involved where an identical make of car is not used on a flow-line. Here is a suggested service whihc has been used successfully.

Commercial vehicle standard service

1. Check rear axle and gear box, oil levels, top up as necessary. Visual inspection of suspension. Check wheel nuts.
2. Change engine oil and filters. Check fan belt and engine generally.
3. Jack up, check brakes and steering. Check lights and focus headlamps.
4. Check fifth wheel coupling and all fittings. Check tyres for pressure and for cracks, loose bolts etc.
5. Full lubrication of all grease and oil points. Check tyres for pressure and wear.
6. Smoke check.

Now these items need to be completed at six stages as indicated, each stage in this case taking about 30 minutes—a total of 3 hours. The line could be arranged as shown in Fig. 1.5 but such is not essential. In practice a line can operate by driving a vehicle from one bay area to another as shown in Fig. 1.6. Pits or lifts are required to carry out the service.

In Fig. 1.7 a further flow-line is shown to give an idea of variations that can be adopted.

At some service stations only one make of car is taken on the line. In addition to the usual service requirements many additions are made, making it

FLOWLINE FOR COMMERCIAL VEHICLES

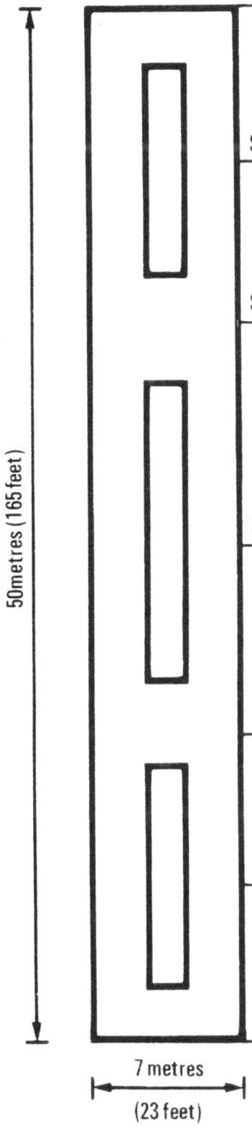

LINE	STAGES	EQUIPMENT	STAFF
	STAGE 1	(a) LIFT OR PIT (b) TOOLS FOR JOBS	1 SEMI-SKILLED MECHANIC
	STAGE 2	TOOLS FOR JOB	1 SKILLED MECHANIC
	STAGE 3	(a) TROLLEY JACK OR WHEEL FREE LIFT (b) STEERING ALIGNMENT EQUIPMENT (c) HEADLAMP ALIGNMENT EQUIPMENT (d) TOOLS FOR JOB	1 SKILLED MECHANIC 1 UNSKILLED WORKER
	STAGE 4	(a) LIFT OR PIT (b) TOOLS FOR JOB	1 SKILLED MECHANIC
	STAGE 5	(a) LUBRICATION EQUIPMENT (b) LIFT OR PIT (c) AIRLINE FOR TYRES (d) TOOLS FOR JOB	1 SEMI-SKILLED MECHANIC
	STAGE 6	SMOKE METER	1 SEMI-SKILLED MECHANIC

50 metres (165 feet)

7 metres (23 feet)

Fig. 1.5 Flow-line Layout (1)

very attractive to customers. This service is shown below and the work is executed in 6 stages as follows:

Stage 1. Remove wheels. Inspect tyres for wear and report. Balance wheels. Check tyre pressure. Check brake adjustments, mechanisms and linings.

Inspect drums, discs and leaks from hub seals. Inspect dampers, road springs, Hydrolastic units, swivel pins. Replace wheels and check that they rotate freely. Check under bonnet. Adjust tappets and pull down cylinder head if required. Renew valve cover gasket. Clean or renew air cleaner element as required. Check fan belt condition and adjust.

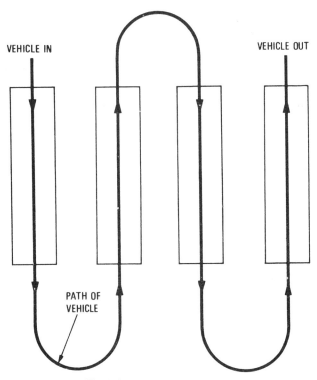

Fig. 1.6 Flow-line Layout (2)

Stage 2. Test braking efficiency (including hand-brake). Check and top up dampers. Tighten carburettor and manifold flanges. Clean or renew distributor points. Check and clean distributor caps and rotor arm, centrifugal spring tension, oil centre spindle. Check and tighten battery connections. Top up battery. Test horn, heater and windscreen wipers. Check seat and window mechanisms, wiper blades and windscreen washers. Check and adjust head-lamp alignment and brilliance. Test all lamps, including indicators, interior lights and panel warning lamps. Lubricate door locks and hinges.

Stage 3. Clean or change plugs. Check compressions on engine and test cylinder head gasket for leaks. Test pressure system in radiator, all connections and hoses and top up if required. Top up windscreen-washer bottle. Check brake and clutch master cylinders and slave cylinder. Check and adjust clutch pedal. Check safety belt anchorages. Test for oil, petrol and water leaks throughout

Commercial Vehicle Flow-Line

Line	Stages	Equipment and Service	Staff
	Stage 1	Pit for full lubrication and chassis inspection	1 skilled Mechanic 1 semi-skilled Mechanic
	Stage 2	Area only for oil filter change on engine and general engine check	1 skilled Mechanic
	Stage 3	Coupling check, cab and body check, headlamp alignment Area and headlamp equipment	1 skilled Mechanic
	Stage 4	Steering and brake check Area and equipment	1 skilled Mechanic 1 unskilled Mechanic
	Stage 5	Quality control check for power output on dynamometer. Smoke meter check	1 skilled Mechanic
	Stage 6	Wash with vehicle washer polish	1 unskilled worker

Note. **Stage 6** can be suitably placed at **Stage 1**. DOE work demands top and under cleaning. Thus, washing underneath before inspections is really essential.

Fig. 1.7 Flow-line Layout (3)

vehicle. Test exhaust system and tighten brackets. Check pipes, cables, propeller shaft couplings and bell ends. Check and top up oil and fluid levels in engine, gearbox, rear axle, brake master cylinder, clutch master cylinder, idler box, steering box, rack and pinion and automatic. Lubricate grease points, dynamo, bearing and water pump. Change oils if instructed.

Stage 4. Adjust throttle and choke controls. Test battery voltage, cranking voltage, starter system, charging voltage and voltage regulator. Check coil voltage, voltage drop, points, primary windings in coil. Test distributor, condenser, coil polarity and secondary windings. Check h.t. leads, plugs. Adjust ignition timing. Check automatic advance, vacuum advance, centrifugal-advance, and air/fuel ratios at idle, intermediate and high speeds. Check power in each cylinder.

Stage 5. Test road performance. Acceleration test. Overrun test 100 kilometres per hour to 65 kilometres per hour (60 miles per hour to 40 miles per hour approximately). Record maximum power reading and speed in top gear. Test fuel consumption at 70 kilometres per hour (45 miles per hour). Check accuracy of speedometer at varying speeds. Test clutch operation, differential operation and engine rev/min.

Stage 6. Full wash.

In all these flow-lines, equipment to operate the service is placed at suitable points along the line to enable the work at the various stages to be completed. Equipment for one Service of B.L.M.C. cars is arranged as shown in Fig. 1.8 but not in the straight line shown because of space difficulties.

A final example is shown in Fig. 1.9.

A standard service for any make of car is shown now. Care should be taken in planning the line to avoid bottlenecks as previously explained.

Standard service for cars and light vans

1. Check steering and wheel alignments.
2. Check brakes and adjust as necessary.
3. Check engine for loose, worn components, fan belt. Adjust as necessary.
4. Check plugs and points. Clean and reset. Electronic engine analyser check.
5. Full lubrication service.
6. Check chassis and body generally for deterioration.
7. Check suspension.

Diagnostic centres

Diagnostic Centres have been in operation in the U.S.A. a decade and have become popular in this country where they have been well promoted. Such centres not only diagnose faults as a normal rule, they are also used to check work done on a car as a means of quality control in the workshop. Diagnosis is made by performing inspections to discover what parts of a car or commercial vehicle require adjustment or repair. It is a useful aid to generate more

Line	Stage	Equipment	Staff
Automatic Door Path of Car 50 metres	**Stage 1** All gaskets, parts etc. placed in a basket inside the car	Wheel free lift Wheel balancer Torque wrench and other suitable tools	One skilled Mechanic One semi-skilled Mechanic
	Stage 2	Brake tester Headlamp alignment equipment Tools as required	2 Mechanics
	Stage 3	One lift or pit Compression tester Radiator and cap tester Tools as required	1 Mechanic 1 unskilled worker
	Stage 4	Electronic engine analyser Tools as required	1 skilled Mechanic
	Stage 5	Dynamometer	1 skilled Mechanic
5 metres Wash-Finish	**Stage 6**	Car washing machine	1 unskilled operator

Fig. 1.8 Diagnostic Flow-line Service Layout

This line not only 'services' a car but many extra items are checked on the cars. 'Diagnosing' or 'fault finding' are part of the line. The customer can benefit by having defective parts replaced after service and not whilst out on the road! Because of diagnostic checks with servicework it would be true to say that this arrangement is *A Diagnostic Flow-Line Service Layout*. Staff are fully utilized for skill and time thus aiding efficiency and profitability.

business in the workshop. When diagnostic equipment is used as a means of quality control, any repairs executed are tested to ensure the finished job is satisfactory and operation is within certain limits. For example, if new contact breaker points have been fitted and the dwell angle is 57°–63° then the quality control check should reveal whether the mechanic has completed the work satisfactorily. Most jobs can be checked with correct type of equipment.

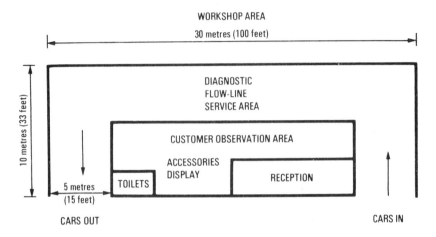

Fig. 1.9 Diagnostic Flow-line Service Layout

Note: 1) Difficult corners to negotiate—not recommended.
2) Lifts placed in such a way cars cannot be shunted off the line if a serious defect is found.
3) For preference a 6 metre width is desired so that cars on minor or major service can proceed to sections of a line or to enable one section to be omitted.
4) A flow-line can be operated for part of a working day if considered suitable for prevailing custom and conditions.
5) As with repair work, cars should be serviced away from commercial vehicles. Otherwise, car owning customers may expect damage to occur.

From the garage point of view advantages of diagnostic centres are as follows:
1) Equipment installed is useful for diagnostic and quality control.
2) Faults revealed are generally passed to the workshop thus increasing profit on labour and parts.
3) It is attractive to customers who appreciate checks for safety and efficiency.
4) Flexibility for partial inspections if of a bay type centre.
5) Use for checking second-hand vehicles prior to repair and selling.

14627101

The disadvantages from the garage owner's point of view could be summarized as follows:

1) Costly investment.
2) Mechanics have to be trained to use the equipment.
3) Space taken which otherwise could be used for repair bays.

However, all of these disadvantages can be nullified provided the centre is a well advertised in a reasonable area where car population is good, and gives an efficient service to attract customers back time and time again. Some service stations run diagnostic clubs offering two or three diagnostic checks per year for a fixed fee of £10 or so.

If it is decided to proceed with a diagnostic centre, the next decision is what type of layout should be considered. Space is the all-important factor but at least one of the layouts below will be suitable.

1) A diagnostic lane with inspection stations end to end for drive-through operation. This usually takes in a service as well as a diagnostic check but can be used for a diagnostic lane only. It does, however, require a sizeable investment and constant promotion to achieve a profitable throughput of of cars. It is not suitable for partial inspections and is not adaptable to general repair work. On the other hand, a large volume of work does mean large profits. Operators of such lanes without rivals have found that some 200 000 car registrations are required within a ten mile radius to keep the lane busy.

2) A bay set up where the diagnostic equipment is arranged in one or more stalls. This idea is very popular but does not have the potential of business as the lane method. It does however result in less investment and performs the same task as a lane. It can also be used as a quality control bay. Bays can be added as required.

3) A diagnostic service with existing facilities. Here a section of a workshop is made into a diagnostic area using existing equipment and space. Equipment can be supplemented as required. If this produces the custom a separate diagnostic bay can be installed at a later date.

Equipment for diagnostic centres

The equipment needed for any centre will depend upon the service offered. For a comprehensive diagnostic check the following equipment will be required.

Wheel-free lift/s, comprehensive electronic engine analysing equipment, headlamp alignment equipment, comprehensive wheel alignment equipment, wheel balancer, chassis dynamometer and brake tester, services to operate this equipment (air, electricity and water). This comprises all major equipment. In the future it is likely to be extended to include front wheel dynamic steering checks. This involves running the front wheels on rollers that can swivel and thus check the steering mechanisms. Likewise, mechanical tests on dampers (shock-absorbers) will be made. In the U.S.A. some tests of this nature are

A /658.92

already completed along with such things as chemical analysis of automatic gear-box oils to determine whether the oil is contaminated and the type and amount of wear this could indicate.

In addition to the major items listed additional diagnostic service tools required are as follows: Brake drum micrometer, Calipers to measure brake lining thickness, cooling system and pressure cap tester also antifreeze tester, tyre tread depth gauge and tyre pressure gauge, height gauges for measuring torsion bar and spring heights, ball joint checking instrument, torque wrenches for various parts, air cleaner tester and hand tools as required.

Recently developed equipment which will probably find its way into diagnostic centres and now used in repair shops is the sonic leak tester. This quickly tests and traces leaks in brakes lines; slow punctures and body leaks can also be very quickly detected. Thus, a quick check of braking systems for slight leaks is possible and another addition to any diagnostic centre.

Washing and car valeting

Very recently car washers have become very popular in the retail motor trade. Washers of course are not new but certain events have taken place which must now make good car washers a part of any good service station layout.

Let us examine the reasons for investing in such equipment. First, the general public are beginning to shrink from the time-consuming messy job of washing the car as a Sunday ritual. Many people are more interested in leisure than in washing cars. Representatives, executives and many more people cannot spare the car for one to three hours and are anxious to have a clean car in 3 minutes or 10 minutes depending on the type of wash being made. Before the car wash is installed, a service manager will have a good idea of its possible use by assessing car population, existing customers, competition already in the area and so on. Use of the car wash could form part of the end of a flow-line or it could be used before any car is serviced, thus helping to keep the workshop clean and customers satisfied. With relatively low cost washing, custom must grow. A car wash then can be useful as a profitable side-line and as an aid to efficient workshop practice. Like all equipment, however, it must pay its way and budgeted for accordingly.

There are a number of washers available and selection must meet the needs of the service station where it is to be installed. Let us examine typical installations.

Coin operated car wash

With one attendant this wash proceeds as follows:
1) Coins or tokens are inserted in the meter which is positioned so that the driver need not get out of his car.
2) Red light changes to green indicating driver to proceed to a marked spot.
3) Conveyor chain is switched on by the vehicle by a contact switch and vehicle is pushed forward.

4) Shampoo spray arch loosens road film and dirt.
5) Brushing stage where 7 brushes move over the car, 2 on the wheels, 4 on
   the sides and 1 on the roof. Brushes are self-cleaning thus avoiding streaks
   on the paintwork.
6) As the car moves along parts of it are washed several times by different
   jets placed in different positions.
7) Rinsing arch—vehicle rinsed with water.
8) Wax spraying arch—vehicle paintwork fully sprayed with wax emulsion.
9) Vehicle rolls into drying zone which is completely separated by a special
   anti-splash door and which does not open until touched by the front of
   the vehicle. High air pressure and air speed quickly dry the car avoiding
   streaks on the paint work. The horizontal air jets are suspended telescopi-
   cally and glide close to the vehicle contours guided by photo-cell scan-
   ning. Other air jets are placed in suitable vertical positions.
10) A second green light comes on indicating the car can leave the wash—
    finished!

It takes two weeks to install this wash. The wash itself takes 3 minutes and
60 cars per hour can use the wash. The inside of the car is not cleaned but
some service stations now have valeting for the inside as well; we shall discuss
this later.

Fixed-car moving-gantry car wash

With this type of wash, the car remains stationery whilst a gantry on rails
moves over the car, cleaning the car in a similar way to the wash described
above. Certain items operate differently and the process could consist of
clean water wash, detergent wash, rinse and dry without waxing.

Wall-mounted container wash

Simple car washers are still available which consists of a wall mounted con-
tainer which has an electrically driven pump. The pump operates at pressures
up to $3.12N/mm^2$ ($450lbf/in^2$). An operating lever with 'Off', 'Detergent' and
'Water Rinse' positions is used by the operator. By directing the jet on to
various parts of the car cleaning is completed. The jet is sometimes replaced
by a brush and mains water pressure only used. The high pressure referred to
is especially useful for cleaning the underneath of cars. Warm of hot water
gives better results with this type of wash which takes between 5 and 10
minutes. Care should be taken to avoid forcing water into door locks where
subsequently it could freeze in cold weather.

Valeting

The washed car can now receive internal valeting (if required) as part of the
service. American car valeting has operated like this for many years. To do

this a good vacuum cleaner is essential. Special car vacuum cleaners are available and these have special nozzles to enable every part of the car to be cleaned thoroughly. Stiff brushes form part of the vacuum nozzles with some makes so that brushing cloth upholstery results in improved cleaning and appearance. An operator is necessary for this job and in some American valeting stations one operator vacuums the car, empties ash-trays front and rear whilst another operator applies a quick silicone polish to any metal parts as well as using a duster to wipe over the instrument panel. Difficult stains on upholstery are not removed in the wash area. The car is shunted off for this work if required and one of the many patented cleaners for leather or P.V.C. used. Upholstery cleaners of this nature have improved greatly in recent years and various cleaners are now available for all types of materials. The American car valeting includes wash, wax, dry, polish, internal vacuum and polish. Taking about 15 minutes and costing up to 2 dollars it is a very popular service in America.

The layout and selection of the car-wash and valeting equipment will depend on seven factors, namely (1) will customers use the wash and car valeting equipment—a survey will indicate this, (2) is the car population sufficient to merit installation, (3) could 'contract' work be obtained from local fleet owners, (4) would the service station 'workshop' and 'car sales' benefit— especially if cars stand outside for sales purposes and a lot of cleaning is involved, (5) what is the cost of running the equipment and is it a profitable proposition, (6) is a good space available to install the wash so that customers can easily see it and use it, (7) what competition exists or is likely to exist in the future?

As with all items of equipment, a careful assessment to make up a profit and loss account should be made prior to purchase. The account, in this case, would include (1) cost of installation and consequent loss of interest on capital invested, (2) cost of running the wash, i.e. electricity, water rate for water used and disposal of effluent from the wash, promotion costs, cost of detergents/waxes, hidden costs such as cleaning out of the water-traps each week, and the need of protection against frost damage if located outside, depreciation costs of equipment on a 5 or 10 year life depending upon the manufacturer of equipment being used and charges for maintenance of equipment.

On the credit side is the customer who pays for individual washes and contract work. Other credits are of course the value to the workshop and car sales in 'time saved' which is always difficult to assess.

Before installing any such equipment a service manager should examine as many car-washes and car valeting items as he can in order to select the equipment best suited to his needs. A student would benefit greatly by visiting service stations which have such equipment and obtaining comprehensive answers to the questions listed below.

· Visit to a car valeting area of a service station

1. How in detail does the car-wash operate, i.e. water used, detergents, wash/ wax times, types of brushes, etc.
2. What quality of finish is obtained when a car comes through the wash and is presented to the customer (water-streaks, brush marks, etc.)? Is it necessary to provide brushes and detergent mixture for parts of the car missed in the wash?
3. What are the costs of installation, cost of running and return on investment expected over one year? Make out a profit and loss account.
4. (a) How would you promote a car wash?
   (b) How does this particular workshop promote the wash?
5. Once the car has been washed the complete valeting includes internal cleaning. Detail the jobs to be done then (a) how you would have them completed? (b) how does this workshop complete the jobs?
6. Why was the car-wash located in this position and what are the advantages and disadvantages of a car-wash on a service station site.

Breakdown equipment

A vehicle which breaks down on the road has to be moved as quickly as possible so that obstruction of the road is reduced to a minimum. The cause of a breakdown could range from a failed capacitor in the ignition system to a collapsed set of gears in a gear-box. Consequently, the mechanics going out on a recovery vehicle must be fully experienced, be able to diagnose faults quickly, be able to use all the recovery equipment (e.g. winch, crane, slings, shackles, tow bar, towing ambulance—a tow bar with wheels and cradle, the broken down vehicle is lifted onto the ambulance at one end and towed using the front or rear wheels of the vehicle as required—, fire extinguisher, first aid and all other appliances on the breakdown vehicle. Recovery crews should also be familiar with the restrictive speeds when towing which vary according to type of recovery vehicle, that is whether solid or pneumatic tyres which have 13 kilometres per hour or 26 kilometres per hour (8 or 16 miles per hour) limits). Breakdown vehicles, fully equipped, are now supplied by manufacturers specializing in this type of vehicle. However, the important thing is to ensure that recovery vehicle mechanics can use the slings and lifting gear safely and are fully aware that a safe working load marked on a lifting item means that this load cannot be exceeded. Thus a crane marked S.W.L. 1 000 kg (2 200 lb) means that nothing can be lifted that will exceed this amount. This also applied to the slings, shackles, hooks and all lifting devices which have a *safe working load* stamped on them or identified by tags attached to them.

When called out, a breakdown crew have to be prepared to pull vehicles out of ditches, tow wrecked vehicles and complete a host of repairs to get a vehicle back into a workshop. The breakdown vehicle should be equipped as stated previously and in addition should have the following: sledge-hammer, crow-bars, a length of rope 30 mm ($1\frac{3}{16}$ in) diameter and 40 metres long (130 feet), two or three wooden planks 80 mm (3 in) thick with widths of 10 cm (4 in), 20 cm (8 in) and 30 cm (12 in), at least 2 metres (6 feet) long, a trolley jack of good capacity, large steel levers, portable electric lamps, locking clamps for a steering wheel when a car has to be towed backwards, flashing beacon to indicate a breakdown, waterproof clothing for the breakdown mechanics, a suitable 'on tow' notice board for attaching to the vehicle, lengths of twin electric cable and spare lamp holders for attaching to the broken down vehicle for rear illumination if required and a normal mechanics' tool-kit. Many garages mark breakdown equipment kept on the vehicle with a special bright paint so that the equipment is kept on the vehicle and does not find its way into the workshop. Periodically, the breakdown vehicle's lifting equipment has to be inspected under the Factories Act, and at the same time it is useful to check that all breakdown equipment is correct by checking the inventory on the vehicle. The inspection of lifting equipment, incidently, is carried out by an independent inspecting engineer usually belonging to an insurance company. A report is then issued and has to be filed by the garage owner for inspection by the Factory Inspector as required. The condition of the equipment is recorded and these reports and any action required should receive immediate attention.

Finally, the size of the breakdown vehicle will depend upon its use. A car recovery vehicle will have a capacity up to 3 000 kg (6 600 lb) and a commercial recovery vehicle at least twice this amount to meet the needs of modern heavy vehicles. Consequently, commercial recovery vehicles often have high capacity engines to give very high tractive effort at their road wheels.

Budgeting—evaluation and selection of workshop equipment

When considering the purchase of equipment the correct approach is *will it pay*? Not *what does it cost*?

When tools or equipment are being thought about as *labour saving* devices, the costing must be marked out on the following lines. Let us assume a power tool is available to replace a hand tool.

Example
a) Cost of hand tool = £6 Power Tool = £60.
b) Cost of operator = £0.5 per hour.
c) Power tool halves job time.
d) Operating time 1 000 hours per year on hand tool.
e) Power consumption 0.5 h.p. per hour.
f) Power cost 1p per h.p. per hour
g) For the hand tool allow *20% of cost* for depreciation, maintenance and other cost. i.e. 20% of £6 = £1.20. Annual labour cost = 1 000 × £0.50 = £500

Running costs of hand tool = £1.20 + £500 =

£501.20

For the power tool allow 10% for maintenance, 10% for depreciation, 3% per annum capital charge (which is the interest which could be obtained by putting the cost of the machine into a safe investment).

a) *Capital charge* interest (3% on £60) = £1.80
b) *Depreciation* (10% of £60) = £6.00
c) *Maintenance* (10% of £60) = £6.00
d) *Power costs* ($\frac{1\,000\ \text{hours}}{2} \times \frac{1\text{p}}{2}$) = £2.50

(half h.p. and half operating time)

e) *Labour* (500 hours × £0.50) = £250

£266.30

Use of hand tool costs £501.20
Use of power tool costs £266.30

£234.90 = *saving in costs per annum.*

Difference means

1) Reduction in price of job possible and a better chance in competition.
2) Increase in general turnover leading indirectly to greater profit.

This calculation assumes that other work would be found for the mechanic during the time saved otherwise labour costs would be the same and extra cost of power would be all loss.

Depreciation of equipment

All equipment wears out and due allowance must be made for this. The same applies to buildings, vehicles and so on. In connection with depreciation the following formulae can be used as a means of calculating annual depreciation.

Let P = original cost of machine, equipment, building etc.

N = number of years of estimated useful life of unit.

R = scrap or second hand value at the end of N years.

D = annual sum to be charged as depreciation.

Thus $D = \dfrac{P - R}{N}$

Example– An electronic engine analyser when purchased cost £1 000 and its useful life is estimated at 5 years. The scrap value of the equipment is expected to be £30. What is the annual depreciation?

$$D = \frac{P - R}{N}$$

$$\therefore D = \frac{1\,000 - 30}{5} = \frac{970}{5} = £194$$

Annual Depreciation = £194.

Depreciation of all garage equipment and assets has to be considered in order to obtain correct profit and loss accounts. Depreciation of different items varies considerably. Here are some approximate rates of depreciation per annum.

Asset	Annual Rate of Depreciation (%)
Buildings	2.5
Boilers	5.0
Electrical cables	3.0
Electrical motors	8.0
Electrical transformers	8.0
Electrical dynamos	8.0
Diesel engines	10.0
Lorries	22.5
Coaches	15.0
Vans	20.0

From experience, depreciation values will vary from these given. For example, a temporary concrete building could depreciate to scrap value between 10 and 20 years. Suppliers will always be pleased to give this information. Similarly, *use* of a machine such as a pillar drill will affect depreciation as well as natural ageing of wiring and insulation. Machines such as drills, lathes, grinders etc. are usually depreciated at a rate of 7.5 to 10.00% per annum, whilst tools are depreciated at a rate of 5.0 per annum. Taking the latter as an example, it means tools should last 20 years before becoming scrap. Mechanics will know that some tools will last longer and some much shorter than this because usage, quality of material as well as natural ageing affect depreciation. Consequently, whilst the formulae and figures given are useful aids to calculating depreciation, the facts regarding the number of years of useful life should be carefully considered in all calculations.

Selection of equipment for a workshop

It will be obvious that the size of the workshop and the amount of work expected will have a strong bearing on the equipment to be purchased. No workshop can be efficient without suitable tools and equipment. The service station owner, service manager or other responsible person will decide which equipment is necessary as an aid to efficiency and profitability in a workshop. An entirely new layout gives a great opportunity for careful selection and placing of equipment to obtain maximum productivity from the repair shop. As stated previously the different types of garages perform servicing and repair operations according to size, and equipment must be of a certain standard if M.A.A. membership is being sought. An independent operator, however, will choose for himself from the tools and equipment listed below what exactly suits his needs.

A list of equipment and tool *suppliers* can always be obtained by looking at trade journals. Two journals which specialize in equipment and tools as well as small technical articles are: *The Service Station* and *Garage and Transport Equipment.*

Motor vehicle workshop equipment

Wheel Free and other types of *Lifts.*
Comprehensive wheel alignment equipment.
Air compressor.
Combined dynamometer and brake tester (or individual units if more suitable).
Lubrication equipment.
Brake servicing equipment.
Wheel balancer.
Lifting jacks.
Paraffin wash tanks and degreasing plant.
Hydraulic press.
Battery charging unit including hydrometer, 0–20 V voltmeter and High Rate Discharge Tester.
Steam cleaner or high pressure water cleaner.
Electrical testing equipment for starters, dynamo, ignition circuits and timing.
Electronic engine analyser equipment (comprehensive).
Power hacksaw.
Comprehensive engine overhaul equipment comprising engine stands, cylinder boring, grinding and re-sleeving plant, valve and valve seat grinding and re-seating equipment, connecting rod alignment jig, piston and piston ring service tools valve spring compressors, various cylinder gauges, micrometers and verniers.
Main bearing and big-end bearing boring equipment.
Tyre repair plant for tubes, valve vulcanizers, also includes tyre removing jig, tyre levers and vulcanizing unit for permanent repairs to tubeless tyres and inner tubes.
Oxyacetylene and metallic arc welding equipment (could include spot welding machine and/or continuous wire feed CO_2 welding equipment).
Headlamp alignment equipment.
Gas soldering ovens and irons with assorted bits.
Lathe, 15 cm to 24 cm (6 in to 9 in) centres with various tools and attachments, e.g. milling head.
Power drills—Bench pillar type with capacity up to 30 mm ($1\frac{1}{4}$ in) diameter drill. Portable drills, capacity up to 15 mm ($\frac{5}{8}$ in) diameter drill.
Power shaping machine (small).
Breakdown and salvage plant usually a vehicle completely equipped with a crane, winch and other tackle.
Shop benching with tool racks and steel tool cupboards and steel vices 7.5 cm and 15 cm jaws (3 in and 6 in).

Creepers for under car work.

Diesel pump and injector testing equipment, also includes reconditioning equipment for injectors and pumps. Smoke tester.

Body Repair Equipment, this can be very extensive, but should include *body jigs* for checking car dimensions, hydraulic push and pull rams with assorted connections and heads, a comprehensive range of dollies and spoons, planishing hammers, sanders (air or electric) buffers and polishers, paint spraying equipment with suitable booths and paint baking ovens. Welding equipment to include oxyacetylene CO_2 Metallic Inert Gas, (MIG) metallic arc and portable spot welding equipment with variety of heads and cranked arms. Sheet metal cutting, folding and rolling equipment. Straight and curved tinsnip.

Forge or hearth can still be useful, but virtually obsolete. However, still essential for much workshop practice is a *gas brazing blowpipe* 2 cm (0.75 in) to use with a *small forge* and *swage block*.

Anvil with tongs (flat and round).

Marking out equipment comprising surface plate, scribing block, steel squares, surface gauges, scribing blocks, dividers, scribers, engineers' blue, sine bar, protractors.

Axle stands for cars and commercial vehicles.

Portable crane or hoists for lifting vehicles or units such as engines.

Fire fighting and first aid equipment.

Bench grinding-machine with coarse and fine stones 20 cm (8 in) diameter.

Shot-blasting cabinet for cleaning parts which have cavities in difficult positions.

Turntables for garages with restricted space.

Sparking plug cleaning and testing machine.

Motor vehicle workshop tools, these are tools normally held in stores or on steel racks for use by mechanics. A comprehensive tool kit for mechanics suggested by the R.T.I.T.B. is given on pages 29 to 31.

Lathe tools, right and left hand assorted cutters, boring tools, screw cutting, knurling and chaser tools.

Drills, assorted from 1 mm to 25 mm ($\frac{1}{32}$ in to 1 in) also drills to suit special thread diameters.

Reamers, taper and parallel, also expanding reamers essential for repair work. Reamer sizes most used range from 10 mm to 30 mm ($\frac{3}{8}$ in to $1\frac{3}{16}$ in).

Sets of screw-cutting dies and taps. Threads to be cut will depend upon choice of dies and taps. Most common for motor vehicle work are metric, U.N.C., U.N.F., B.S.F., B.A. with Whitworth and B.S.P. found occasionally.

Screw thread gauges are kept with these tools also thread restorers.

Hammers various shapes and weights. Steel, leather, copper and rubber faced. Sledge hammers of 4 kilogramme (7 lb) weight is a popular size.

Scrapers of various shapes and sizes for bearing and decarbonizing.

Bolt cutters up to 20 mm ($\frac{3}{4}$ in) capacity.

Torque wrenches with capacity up to 30 NM (120 lbf ft)

Oil cans large and small.

Tyre pressure gauges.
Sets of ring spanners, short and long reach, also open-ended spanners.
Socket spanners. Assorted sockets to suit bolt and nut sizes normally used.
Sets of feeler guages metric and english sizes as required with taper blades.
Portable electric pressurized safety *inspection lamps* with low voltage supply.
Hacksaws with 20 cm to 30 cm (9 in to 12 in) frames.
Extractors for bearings and bolts.
Cold chisels, 5 mm to 30 mm ($\frac{3}{16}$ in to $1\frac{3}{16}$ in) width.
Multi-wheel braces for assorted wheel nuts.

Recommended apprentice tool kit. (R.T.I.T.B.)

(Note: R.T.I.T.B. give English sizes for tools only except for open-end, sockets
and ring spanners listed).

Box,
Tool kit, steel with lock.
Bar,
40 cm Pry (16 in).
Brushes,
Steel wire 2 row,
engine cleaning,
file cleaning.
Chisels,
cold flat,
    crosscut,
      diamond point.
Caliper,
firm joint inside,
        outside.
Drifts,
brass.
Dividers,
16 cm (6 in) Quick release.
Files,

flat safe	bastard 2nd Cut
edge	25 cm (10 in) 20 cm (8 in)
flat edge	15 cm (6 in)
round	20 cm (8 in)
half round	20 cm (8 in)
square	15 cm (6 in)
warding	10 cm (4 in)

Gauges,
engineers' feeler, imperial and metric.

Hammers,
ball pein engineers' 0.75 kg ($1\frac{1}{2}$ lb)
                0.25 kg ($\frac{1}{2}$ lb)
combination hide and copper 1.5 kg (3 lb).
Keys,
hexagonal (Allen type) imperial and metric.
Punches (Engineers')
centre
parallel (Set of 5) 1 mm to 8 mm ($\frac{1}{16}$in to $\frac{5}{16}$in).
Pliers,
Engineers' side cutting,
round or snipe nose,
diagonal nip.
Rules,
stainless steel 16 cm (6 in) and 24 cm (12 in) with in and mm graduations.
Saws (Engineers'),
hacksaw adjustable frame to take 10 in and 12 in blades,
        Junior,
pad handle.
Screwdrivers,
engineers' heavy,
        light
        chubby,
electricians' large,
            small,
cross head nos. 1, 2, 3 blade
and chubby.
Scriber,
Engineers' double point,
one straight and one right,
angled point.
Square,
engineers 16 cm (6 in).
Scraper,
engineers', hand flat.
Snips,
tinmans.
Spanners,
open jawed BSF—BSW $\frac{1}{8}$ in to $\frac{3}{4}$ in
            AF $\frac{3}{8}$ in to $1\frac{1}{16}$ in
            BA 0 to 10
            metric 8 to 22mm
    socket BSF—BSW $\frac{3}{16}$ in to $\frac{3}{4}$ in
            AF $\frac{7}{16}$ in to $1\frac{1}{16}$ in

Ring,
doubled end BSF–BSW $\frac{3}{8}$ in to $\frac{3}{4}$ in
AF $\frac{3}{8}$ in to $1\frac{1}{16}$ in
Metric 10 to 22 mm,
open jawed adjustable, Length 8 in Jaw Opening 1 in.
Wrenches,
Pipe 8 in for $\frac{3}{4}$ in pipe,
Mole Grips.

Inspection and control of tools and equipment

All tools and equipment should be recorded in an inventory. The inventory should detail the date of purchase, supplier and cost. Spaces should be provided to initial inspection date checks. Inspection is to ensure all equipment is correct and in good working order as well as recording any maintenance carried out. Depending on the size of the station 6 monthly or annual checks should be made. See Fig. 1.10 for a 'safety practices check form' which is recommended to service managers by Vauxhall Motors Training School.

Questions

1. As a Service Manager you are given the task of converting part of your Service Department into a flow line system. Describe how you would lay out this new service and how you would redeploy the staff to operate the service. (I.M.I.)
2. The time spent by skilled mechanics at the Parts Counter still appears to be too high in some repair shops. Describe any system that you know which will eliminate this waste of highly-skilled men's time, or at least reduce it to a minimum. (I.M.I.)
3. In recent years Fleet Owners have become more 'service' minded. How would you organize the regular maintenance of a fleet comprising ten cars and forty medium weight commercial vehicles? (I.M.I.)
4. From time to time it is necessary to take a look at the Repair Workshop to ensure that all available space is being profitably used. How would you layout a Workshop measuring 80 feet by 150 feet with entrance and exit both at one end, so that no floor space was wasted? (I.M.I.)
5. Much valuable workshop space is often taken up by vehicles waiting for spare parts. In many cases this should not have been necessary. How would you organize your parts stock and your Reception/Workshop/Parts Department relations in order to cut this waste to the absolute minimum? (I.M.I.)
6. With operating costs continually rising, discuss whether servicing costs could be reduced without reducing the standard of workmanship and without reducing wages. (I.M.I.)
7. Much emphasis has recently been placed on the importance of quick service to customers. Some garages have met this problem by setting up a flow line

SAFETY PRACTICES CHECK FORM

Date . . . .

Item	Available Yes or No	Operation O.K.	Action Taken	Responsibility
Fire Extinguishers				
Water Buckets				
Sand Buckets				
Fireproof Paint Store				
Fireproof Oil Store				
Flash Proof Bulbs				
Steel Dust Bins (Oily Rags Etc.)				
Oxy-Acetylene Gauges				
Oxy-Acetylene Hoses				
Welding Goggles				
Oily Floors				
Jack Stands				
Garage Jacks				
Chain Hoists				
Emery Wheel Guards				
Emery Wheel Goggles				
Belt Guards				
Lift Opening Gates				
Earther Lead Lamps				
Earthed Electrical Tools				
Loose Pit Boards				
Complete First Aid Kit				

Reproduced by kind permission of Vauxhall Motors Co.

Fig. 1.10 Safety Practices Check Form

installation. Describe this method of operation and also an alternative method of obtaining the same results. (I.M.I.)

8. Describe a suitable system of inspection and control for all shop tools and equipment used in a garage. (I.M.I.)

9. As a service manager you are about to take over a newly built Repair Shop. It has an area of 8 000 square feet and lies behind a showroom and petrol station on a main road. Entry is from the main road and there is an *exit only* to a side road. Draw a sketch showing how you would lay out the shop for general servicing for customers and company vehicles. (I.M.I.)

CHAPTER 2

ORGANIZATION OF DEPARTMENTS

Invoicing

The need for speedy invoicing lies in the fact that many customers pay cash for repairs when the car is released from the workshop. Customers with accounts will also wish to have their bills delivered on time. The service station itself relies on prompt payment in order to meet its own bills for wages, materials, overheads and so on. The quicker an invoice is made out and the sooner payment is received cannot be anything but beneficial to the organization. In any case, when bills are delayed unduly, any dispute about items listed can become obscure, especially if more than one repair has been completed in a short space of time. It is grossly inefficient to present any bills in excess of 28 days from the date of service or repair; in effect this is loaning money free of interest.

To achieve rapid invoicing many innovations have been made. Kalamazoo Ltd., have produced three and five card job sets. Manufacturers' Service Schools such as those of Vauxhall Motors, British Leyland and Ford, have produced their individual interpretations of the easy to complete job sets.

One of these 3 part job sets is shown in Fig. 2.1. The three copies are used together. Usually, the reception engineer will make out the work required on the top copy which is recorded on the second and third copies. The customer signs the form approving the work to be done and this is the customer's invoice. Accounts/Cost Office receive the second copy and the third copy goes to the workshop. The last copy is used by the workshop to make out a job card, record parts used and is filed at reception for use as a service follow-up. On the back of this hard copy shown in Fig. 2.2 is printed the job card for use by the foreman and mechanic. Also detailed is a very useful chart for quality control inspection. The body work section can be completed before work commences and can prevent argument about scratches on bodywork whilst the car was in for repair! New car quality control, that for pre-delivery inspection, will require all parts to be examined as listed. Any faults found being corrected before the customer receives the new car. Many dealers give this quality control check as part of a service, thus helping to promote the garage with customers who appreciate such checks. Any repairs required can be noted and the customer advised. Following repair and certain services, the 'road test summary' will be made and finally, the very important, cleanliness check on door handles, steering wheel, carpets, seats, ashtrays, wings, bonnet and screen. Forming as it does, part of the three part job set, invoicing is rapid and it cuts out other paper work. The only extra work is the requisition note from the foreman to the stores and from the stores to the account/costing section where the final bill is prepared.

The five part job set has copies as follows:
1. customer's invoice,
2. job card,
3. stores authority,
4. accounts/costing,
5. spare copy for retention at reception.

This type of invoicing means that one set of writing only is needed initially and this saves considerable time and expense. As stated previously, Kalamazoo Ltd., Northfield, Birmingham, 31, produce the five card job set which has different colours for each sheet so that identification is easy, e.g. blue for top copy for customer's invoice, yellow for job card and so on, depending on the system adopted. The Kalamazoo five part job set is reproduced in Fig. 2.3.

To use this set the procedure is as follows:
1. Reception engineer details work required on top copy and states if 'credit account' or not by deleting appropriate wording. This copy is retained at reception (No. 1).
2. The second and fourth copies which are the job card and stores authority are handed to the workshop foreman for attention as required.
3. Copy No. 3 is passed to Accounts/Costing to await final parts used. This is obtained from the stores from No. 4 copy when the job is complete. Every part used is charged to the customer.
4. The fifth and final copy is retained by the service manager for future feference.

To summarize the five part job set:

No. 1 copy is retained at reception and finally filed if required.

No. 2 copy—goes to the workshop foreman and then to the service manager for labour sales analysis and then filed.

No. 3 copy goes to Accounts/Costing with No. 5, is duly completed as an invoice when all details from No. 2 and No. 4 copies are to hand. Details of the bill are entered in appropriate accounts ledgers prior to dispatch.

No. 4 copy goes to the workshop foreman, then to the stores where all parts are listed and is then forwarded to Accounts/Costing.

No. 5 is sent to Accounts/Costing and is retained as a copy of the invoice to the customer along with No. 4 copy.

So finally—one copy is retained at reception (if required)
two copies are retained at Accounts/Costing
one copy is retained by the service manager
one copy is the invoice for the customer.

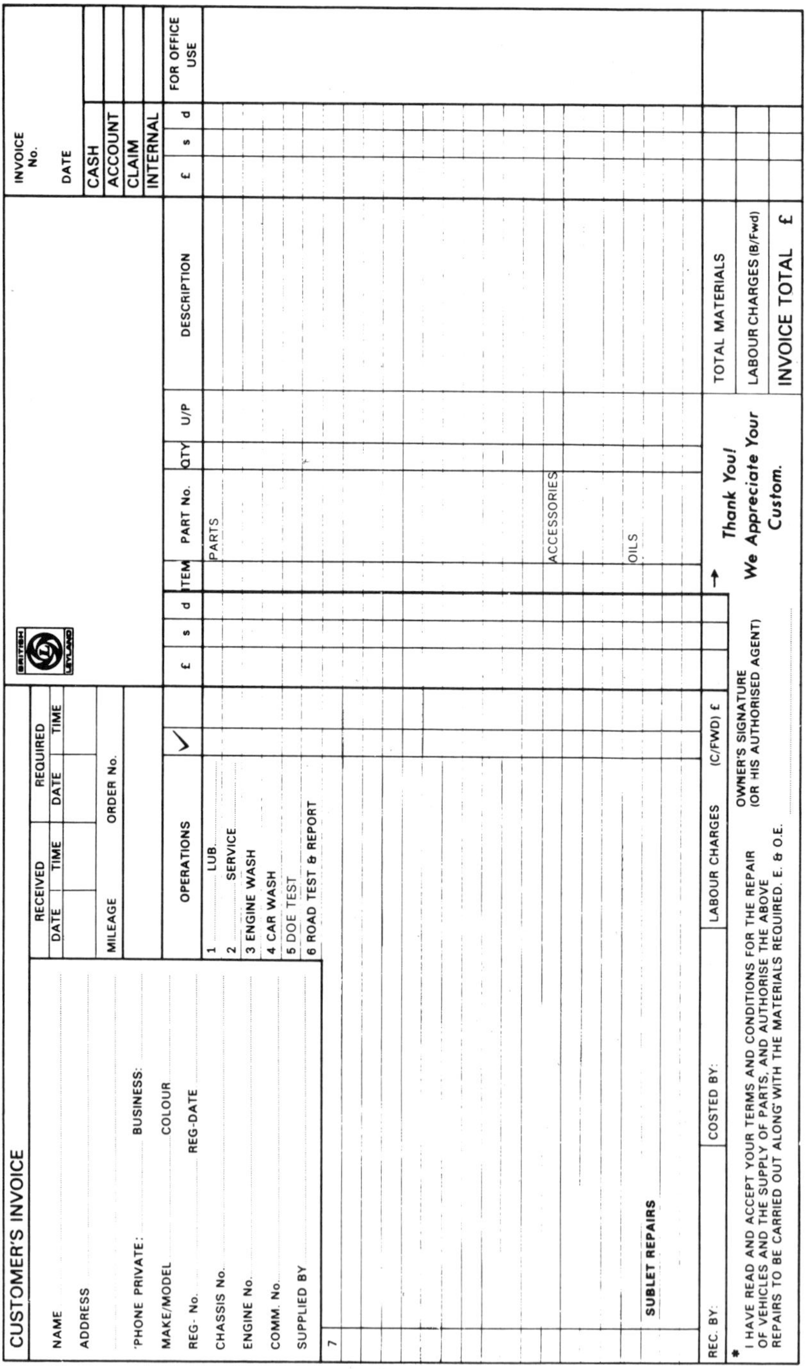

CUSTOMER'S INVOICE

NAME

ADDRESS

'PHONE PRIVATE: BUSINESS:

MAKE/MODEL   COLOUR

REG- No.   REG-DATE

CHASSIS No.

ENGINE No.

COMM. No.

SUPPLIED BY

	RECEIVED		REQUIRED		
	DATE	TIME	DATE	TIME	
MILEAGE			ORDER No.		

ITEM	OPERATIONS		£	s	d
1	LUB.				
2	SERVICE				
3	ENGINE WASH				
4	CAR WASH				
5	DOE TEST				
6	ROAD TEST & REPORT				
7					

SUBLET REPAIRS

COSTED BY: LABOUR CHARGES   (C/FWD) £

REC. BY:

* I HAVE READ AND ACCEPT YOUR TERMS AND CONDITIONS FOR THE REPAIR OF VEHICLES AND THE SUPPLY OF PARTS, AND AUTHORISE THE ABOVE REPAIRS TO BE CARRIED OUT ALONG WITH THE MATERIALS REQUIRED. E. & O.E.

OWNER'S SIGNATURE
(OR HIS AUTHORISED AGENT)

BRITISH LEYLAND

INVOICE No.

DATE

CASH
ACCOUNT
CLAIM
INTERNAL

FOR OFFICE USE

ITEM	PART No.	QTY	U/P	DESCRIPTION	£	s	d
	PARTS						
	ACCESSORIES						
	OILS						

Thank You!
We Appreciate Your Custom.

TOTAL MATERIALS

LABOUR CHARGES (B/Fwd)

INVOICE TOTAL   £

Fig. 2.1 Front of British Leyland 3 Part Job Set

BODYWORK REPORT

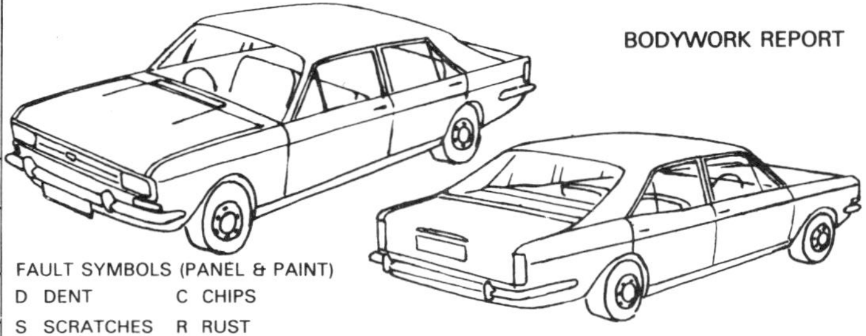

FAULT SYMBOLS (PANEL & PAINT)

D DENT   C CHIPS

S SCRATCHES   R RUST

QUALITY CONTROL INSPECTION

UNDER-BONNET

ENGINE OIL LEVEL/LEAKS	☐	COOLANT/HOSES LEVEL/LEAKS	☐	HYDRAULIC/HOSES LEVEL/LEAKS	☐	BATTERY LEVEL/CORROSION	☐
FAN BELT	☐	FULL THROTTLE CARB DASHPOTS	☐	CHOKE CLOSING	☐	SCREEN WASHER LEVEL	☐

INTERIOR

DOOR HINGES OILED/FREE	☐	COURTESY LIGHT	☐	WARNING LIGHTS INSTRUMENTS HEATER	☐	CHOKE OPERATION SLOW RUNNING	☐
HEADLIGHTS FLASH/DIP	☐	STOP/FLASHER SIDE/REVERSE	☐	SCREEN WASHER WIPER ACTION	☐	FOOT/HANDBRAKE EXCESS TRAVEL	☐

ACCESSORIES

MIRRORS	☐	SPOT/FOG LIGHTS	☐	RADIO	☐	CIGAR LIGHTER	☐

EXTERIOR

DOORS	☐	BONNET	☐	BOOT	☐	WHEEL NUTS	☐
TYRES (INCLUDING SPARE) PRESSURE			☐	CONDITION (TYRES)	☐		

OPERATORS SIGN .... FOREMAN ....

ROAD TEST SUMMARY REF. NO:

ENGINE ....

TRANSMISSION/CLUTCH ....

FINAL DRIVE ....

STEERING/SUSPENSION ....

BRAKES/WHEELS ....

BODY/CHASSIS ....

ELECTRICAL ....

CLEANLINESS DOOR HANDLES ☐ STEERING WHEEL ☐ SEATS/ CARPETS ☐ ASHTRAYS ☐ WINGS ☐ SCREEN ☐

FUEL READING .... TESTERS SIGN. ....

LABOUR

MANS No.	ITEM No.	ELAPSED TIME	TIME	TIME CLOCK RECORD
			OFF	
			ON	
			OFF	
			ON	
			OFF	
			ON	
			OFF	
			ON	
			OFF	
			ON	
			OFF	
			ON	
			OFF	
			ON	
TOTAL				

MATERIALS

REQ. No.

LABOUR

MANS No	ITEM No	ELAPSED TIME	TIME	TIME CLOCK RECORD
			OFF	
			ON	
			OFF	
			ON	
			OFF	
			ON	
			OFF	
			ON	
			OFF	
			ON	
			OFF	
			ON	
			OFF	
			ON	

Fig. 2.2 Back of British Leyland 3 Part Job Set

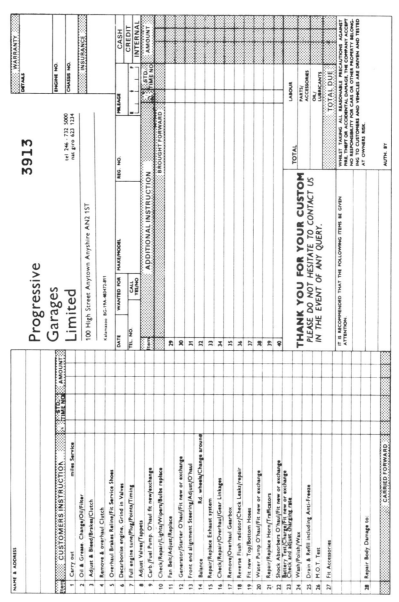

Fig. 2.3 Kalamazoo 3 Part Job Set

Obviously, this procedure can be varied to suit the needs of each particular station. No. 1 copy is only needed at reception as long as the job is in hand and upon dispatch of the job it could be filed in Accounts/Costing with No. 4 and No. 5. These copies are needed where monthly accounts are kept so that customers can be reminded if payment is not forthcoming within 7–14 days of dispatch of the invoice to the customer.

Costing

Sales are vital to profit and so are expenses; they are necessary in order to do business. Expenses, however, have to be controlled and, as will be seen elsewhere in the chapter, they have to be recorded daily, totalled weekly and monthly. Costing, accounting, book-keeping are complicated subjects and this section of the book can only outline the principles involved. Each manager of each department will be responsible for its profitability and recording of sales and expenses will indicate a profit or loss. The modern practice is to allocate a proportionate amount of overheads and other costs to each department according to floor space occupied. Before labour costs can be charged to a customer the actual labour charge is calculated from the amount of overheads and other costs involved so that a profit is made on the sale of labour. The objects of a costing system is to provide accurate information for estimates and repairs, to compare the costs to prices in detail and to show the true earning capacity of each department. With such accurate data we can ensure each job can be made to pay without overcharging. Likewise, unprofitable jobs involving loss or waste are clearly indicated and can be avoided in future work. When departmental expenses are fairly distributed, flat rate prices can be established for many jobs and similar jobs will have similar prices thus avoiding suspicion from customers. Such are the objects and advantages of a costing system.

To assess the profitability of a department costs and expenses must first be placed under two separarate headings i.e. (1) *Direct costs* which include mechanics' wages, materials used for repair work such as parts, cleaning materials and so on: these can be accurately charged to each department according to amount being used. (2) *Indirect costs* which are referred to as 'overheads': these include rental costs, payment of rates, non-productive but essential labour costs such as office staff, advertising etc.

Before we itemize all the costs involved let us consider how each department will have such costs distributed to them.

Each department of a service station will occupy a certain ground area, for example, workshop 800 square metres, (950 square yards), stores 100 square metres, (120 square yards), car showroom 160 square metres (200 square yards), and so on. The total area of all departments may be 1 600 square metres (1 900 square yards). In this case the workshop would pay $\frac{800}{1600}$ of overheads that is 50%. In proportion to area each department can then be similarly assessed. However, some open parking areas will not have to pay the same rates as buildings and must be reduced accordingly, say to half or one third of their share of the indirect costs and all their direct costs, thus obtaining total costs involved.

If we take the workshop quoted as having to pay half the total indirect costs, then if the rates for the buildings were £60 then the workshop must pay £30, the stores (100 × £60)/1 600 = £3.75. How much use is made of office staff and buildings will again be proportioned to the workshop, stores, car sales etc. unless each of these is self contained. In this case they will have their own direct and indirect costs. Overheads can also be apportioned according to capital investment of buildings and equipment and/or number of employees in each department but the area method is most popular with service stations.

Having seen how overheads are allocated, the actual overheads for a garage could include the following: rates, rent, electricity—power and lighting, government taxes, heating, water, advertising, insurance, licences, R.T.I.T.B. levy, depreciation of buildings and equipment, office wages and paper costs, national health insurance contributions, telephone bills and maintenance of buildings will also have to be included. All these items would give a total 'overheads' cost. All known facts must be considered to give a fair distribution of these costs to each department. For example, cost of lighting at night to advertise a showroom and use of toilets by customers. The first will generally be allocated to the showroom overheads and as toilets are usually in the forecourt area, then the forecourt overheads must meet this cost.

Now the usual way to recover these overheads is to apply the formula:

$$\frac{\text{total establishment expenses} \times 100}{\text{total chargeable wages}}$$

The establishment expenses include rent, rates, advertising etc. To check overhead charges, which are passed on to the customer, this formula would be used. For example, if total expenses per annum were £20 000 and total wages £10 000, then overhead charges would be calculated thus:

$$\frac{£20\,000 \times 100}{10\,000} = 200\%.$$

A workshop will recover overheads by applying the formula:

$$\frac{\text{workshop share of overheads} \times 100}{\text{labour costs.}}$$

If the workshop overheads were £100 per month and labour costs were £100 per month, then the percentage on the customers bill to cover the overheads would be (100 × 100)/100 = 100%. Thus if a man is paid £1 per hour and completes 4 hours work on a customer's car, the total cost to the customer would be 4 × £1 + 100% labour cost to meet overheads = £8. This would cover the employment of the man plus all other costs. To make a profit on labour, then a further percentage is added e.g. 100%. In this case the customer would pay £4 for mechanics wages, £4 for overheads, £4 for profit—a total labour charge of £12, i.e. £3 per hour. The profit addition on labour and materials usually averages at 25% so that a competitive labour charge is established. Having achieved the all round rate then a fixed charge for labour is established. Thus, paying a mechanic £1 per hour plus 100% overheads = £2 per hour, plus 25% profit, total labour charge per hour = £2.50. The number of hours on a job is recorded on the job card and on a Pay Claim Slip Form as shown in Fig. 2.4 to enable the wages of a mechanic to be calculated.

Referring to distribution of overheads again, for example to the car sales, they must ensure that sales will cover their share of the overheads as well as a suitable profit margin. About 20% profit on car sales is expected which results in a good net profit on turnover along with a suitable return on capital invested.

A typical Service Department Balance Sheet is shown in Fig. 2.5 which gives a final net profit or loss at the foot of the page. All the expenses listed are self explanatory but one or two items need more details. For instance, 'non-productive time' means time paid to mechanics for 'idle time' when no jobs are available or for correcting faulty work. Other non-productive labour charges are involved when apprentices attend technical college, staff are on courses, holidays with pay and sickness pay, maintenance of break-down vehicle etc. all mean that 100% labour is virtually impossible. If 75% total labour time is acheived this is considered satisfactory, although 100% should always be the aim. Where a time-saved bonus scheme is in operation a minimum labour efficiency is 120%. This must always be carefully watched by the service manager as undue non-productive time is going to affect the profitability of the workshop. Due allowance is sometimes made for unavoidable slack periods in the costing charge for labour by including 25% of the mechanics' wages in the overheads. A daily sales record can be kept by the service manager similar to that used by the Chrysler Co. (U.S.A.) in Fig. 2.6. The Chrysler Co. recommend a 'Monthly Service Department Expense Control Sheet' as shown in Fig. 2.7. The daily chart is completed from the Job Cards and the monthly chart is a total of the daily charts. As monthly charts are maintained a year by year check can be made each and every month to see how the garage is progressing and action can be taken as required.

To return to the costing of a job bearing in mind the points raised, the actual costing is completed by a cost clerk. As stated previously, certain repeat jobs will have standard prices and a typical standard price list offered by one large service station in 1969 is shown in Fig. 2.8. Needless-to-say, this will require modifying as labour charges, taxes, and other prices increase and need to be passed onto the customer. It is, however, much easier to modify such lists and certainly it avoids haphazard costing which can result in different prices for the same job! Manufacturers' Service and Repair Schedules also form a valuable aid to pricing a job. So many hours are allowed by manufacturers for certain services and repair jobs. These have been very carefully analysed by work study methods and give a very fair number of labour hours for a particular job. They are not always available for each job however and, in this case, the job has to be carefully costed to ensure a profit. With such

PAY CLAIM SLIP

TO COST OFFICE DAILY

EMPLOYEE'S NAME						NO	DATE	
N.R. Hours	Std. & T.T. Hours	Item Comp	Item No.	Job No.	Clock No.		Date	
					OFF			
Auth. by					ON			
					Time Taken			
N.R. Hours	Std. & T.T. Hours	Item Comp	Item No.	Job No.	Clock No.		Date	
					OFF			
Auth. by					ON			
					Time Taken			
N.R. Hours	Std. & T.T. Hours	Item Comp	Item No.	Job No.	Clock No.		Date	
					OFF			
Auth. by					ON			
					TimeTaken			
N.R. Hours	Std. & T.T. Hours	Item Comp	Item No.	Job No.	Clock No.		Date	
					OFF			
Auth. by					ON			
					Time Taken			
N.R. Hours	Std. & T.T. Hours	Item Comp.	Item No.	Job No.	Clock No.		Date	
					OFF			
Auth. by					ON			
					Time Taken			
N.R. Hours	Std. & T.T. Hours	Item Comp	Item No.	Job No.	Clock No.		Date	
					OFF			
Auth. by					ON			
					Time Taken			

TOTAL	TOTAL	Adj.Hrs. Plus or Minus		TOTAL ATTENDANCE HOURS		
Col.1	Col.2	Col.3	Col.4	PAY	O/TIME	AUTHORISED

Fig. 2.4 Mechanics' Pay Slip Form

SERVICE DEPARTMENT
PROFIT AND LOSS ACCOUNT

	Current Month	Cumu-lative	LAST YEAR Month	Cumu-lative
	£	£	£	£
RECEIPTS				
Repair Charges —Customer				
—Departmental				
—Warranty Claims				
Engine Department Sales				
Sub Contract Recharged				
Profit on Petrol Sales				
Discount on Parts Sold				
EXPENSES				
Productive Wages				
Deduct: Non productive labour				
Managers and Foremans Salary				
Reception and Tester				
Apprentices				
Tool Stores and Cleaner				
Selective Employment Tax				
N.H.I. & G.P. (Employers Contribution)				
Engine Department Materials				
Sub Contract Charges				
General Time and Works Expenses				
Breakdown and Managers Car Expenses				
Minimum Warranty				
Service Office Salaries				
Total Direct Expenses				
Electricity Gas and Fuel				
General Overhead Apportionment				
TOTAL EXPENSES				
NET PROFIT/(LOSS)				

Fig. 2.5 Service Department Balance Sheet

DAILY SALES RECORD

MONTH_____

DAILY SALES OBJECTIVE	
CUSTOMER LABOR	PARTS
$	$

DATE	NO. CUSTOMER REPAIR ORDERS	CUSTOMER LABOR		PARTS SALES ON R.O.	
		ACCUMULATIVE		ACCUMULATIVE	
		OBJECTIVE	ACTUAL	OBJECTIVE	ACTUAL
1					
2					
3					
4					
5					
6					
7					
8					
9					
10					
11					
12					
13					
14					
15					
16					
17					
18					
19					
20					
21					
22					
23					
24					
25					
26					
27					
28					
29					
30					
31					

Fig. 2.6 A Daily Labour Sales Record (Chrysler)

cases the procedure would be as follows:

1. Customer signs for work to be done. This is very important as (a) it is proof the owner authorized work to be done (b) it authorizes a road test if necessary (c) in the event of death or injury it may be necessary evidence for insurance or workmen's compensation.

2. An estimate of time can either be taken from a similar job completed previously by reference to old job cards or by consultation with the shop foreman. Retail cost of parts are added to the estimates. This will be completed by the reception engineer. The estimate should always be above that amount expected but not excessively high.

3. When the job card is completed and total hours and parts used are listed

MONTHLY SERVICE DEPARTMENT EXPENSE CONTROL

EXPENSE ITEM		JAN	FEB	MAR	APR	MAY	JUN	JUL	AUG	SEP	OCT	NOV	DEC
SALARIES AND WAGES—SERVICE DEPARTMENT	FORECAST												
	ACTUAL												
SUPPLIES AND SMALL TOOLS	FORECAST												
	ACTUAL												
POLICY ADJUSTMENT— SERVICE AND PARTS	FORECAST												
	ACTUAL												
ADVERTISING— SERVICE AND PARTS	FORECAST												
	ACTUAL												
LAUNDRY SERVICE	FORECAST												
	ACTUAL												
MAINTENANCE MACHINERY AND EQUIPMENT	FORECAST												
	ACTUAL												
VACATIONS AND TIME- OFF PAY	FORECAST												
	ACTUAL												
COMPANY CAR EXPENSE	FORECAST												
	ACTUAL												

Fig. 2.7 Chrysler Service Dept. Monthly Expense Control Sheet

by the mechanic, the card is passed to the cost clerk.

4. The cost clerk then totals all labour costs, part costs and, as previously explained, obtains the final charge for detailing on the customers invoice.

5. The invoice or bill is a statement of work done and should clearly state the actual work done. The invoice layout is shown in this chapter. Where a 'one off' job is completed the invoice should include in the description of the work done a concise account of the operations completed along with the cost of each operation. For example:

1100 AND 1300 BMC CARS FIXED PRICE REPLACEMENT SCHEME

Brake System

1 Reline front brakes	5	35	30 Adjust throttle linkage	1	10
2 Reline rear brakes	6	30	31 Throttle cable	1	55
3 Reline all brakes	11	60	32 Tighten all engine nuts and bolts	1	40
4 Clean & abrade front brakes	1	30	33 Tighten all gearbox nuts & bolts	0	85
5 Clean & abrade rear brakes	3	20	34 One drive shaft coupling rubber	4	25
6 Clean & abrade all brakes	4	50	35 Remote control adaptor	2	75
7 Free handbrake mechanism	2	50	**Cooling System**		
8 One brake drum	3	80	36 Fan belt	1	10
9 One brake disc	4	20	37 Top radiator hose	1	20
10 One front wheel cylinder			38 Bottom radiator hose	1	65
11 One rear wheel cylinder	4	15	39 Water pump by-pass hose	4	55
12 Overhaul one brake calliper	3	20	40 Treat with bluecol	1	10
13 Brake master cylinder	4	45	41 Flush out bluecol	0	55
Electrical System			**Suspension: Steering**		
14 Fit one bulb & check wiring	0	30	42 Steering column bushes	2	10
15 Indicator switch	4	50	43 Check and adjust hydrolastic pressures	1	80
16 Adjust indicator switch	0	55	44 Electronic steering check	1	65
17 Decorrode battery	1	65	45 One new tyre – standard	6	70
18 Battery earth lead	0	65	46 Front wheel bearings – one side	4	50
19 Battery negative lead	1	75	47 Rear wheel bearings – one side	4	30
20 Battery jumper lead			48 One front hub oil seal	2	05
21 Battery clamps	0	55	49 One rear hub oil seal	1	25
22 Charge battery	0	85	50 One half shaft gasket		
23 H T distributor leads	1	85	**General**		
24 Distributor rotor arm	0	35	51 One wiper blade	0	70
25 Distributor cap	2	60	52 Adjust w/washer jets	0	30
Engine			53 W/washer control pump	1	95
26 Distributor contact points	1	10	54 Clean out w/washer lines	0	85
27 Engine sparking plugs(set)	1	20	55 Exhaust bracket	1	15
28 Strip clean adjust one carb	1	10	56 Complete exhaust system	6	70
29 Overhaul one carburettor	4	20	57 Reposition exhaust system	0	85

Fig. 2.8 Standard Price List for Replacement of Units

Description of work

Job No.	Labour	Price
28	Removing and dismantling steering box, clean and examine parts	£1.75
	Replace cam and peg mechanism, thrust races, re-assemble and adjust	£0.75
	Refit steering box to car, refill with oil, test	£1.13
	Parts and materials	
	1 cam and peg assembly	£2.75

Job No.   *Labour*   *Price*

2 thrust races		£0.75
1 gasket		£0.07
1 pint S.A.E. 80 oil		£0.20
		£7.40

In the event of a dispute with a customer, the invoice is an essential part of a service station's evidence.

Thus, a job is costed through a garage and a typical repair order flow is shown in Fig. 2.9.

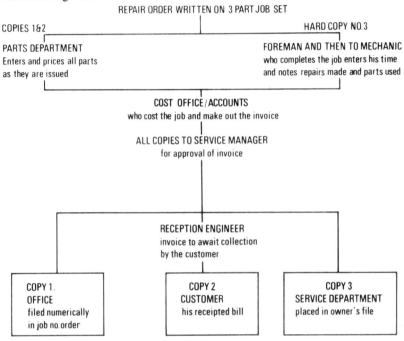

REPAIR ORDER WRITTEN ON 3 PART JOB SET

COPIES 1&2   HARD COPY NO.3

PARTS DEPARTMENT   FOREMAN AND THEN TO MECHANIC
Enters and prices all parts   who completes the job enters his time
as they are issued   and notes repairs made and parts used

COST OFFICE/ACCOUNTS
who cost the job and make out the invoice

ALL COPIES TO SERVICE MANAGER
for approval of invoice

RECEPTION ENGINEER
invoice to await collection
by the customer

COPY 1.   COPY 2   COPY 3
OFFICE   CUSTOMER   SERVICE DEPARTMENT
filed numerically   his receipted bill   placed in owner's file
in job no. order

Variations to the above procedure can be made as required but this
is a typical method of handling repair in a dealership

Fig. 2.9 Repair Order Flow Layout

All consumable items are costed as shown. Control of these items is made by having a signed requisition to the storeman and he in turn makes out the parts issued on the appropriate form—which is passed to the costing section. The storeman is responsible for recording receipt of such items and the issue of parts and this is dealt with in a separate part of this chapter. All parts are received by the garage at a trade price and sold at a profit at a retail price to the customer. Part sales are credited to the Parts Department for their Profit and Loss Account.

Accounts department

The keeping of good and accurate accounts is essential to enable any business to function efficiently. In a large dealership the complete presentation of accounts to auditors and for other purposes, is usually under the control of a qualified accountant. The accountant will have the responsibility of making out the Profit and Loss accounts for each department of the concern, collecting all such information together and finally presenting a Profit and Loss account for the entire firm. These accounts will normally be made up each month with an annual account to cover the years' trading. To obtain this all expenses and receipts are listed. As stated previously, the use of monthly trading accounts from each department enables a quick check to be made on profitability of a particular section. Thus, a full years trading account could indicate a loss even though say, two departments were successful and one unsuccessful. The remedy is obvious and action must be taken to correct the cause of failure in the department concerned.

Organization and administration of the parts department

The size of a dealership will determine whether the parts department has a separate manager or not. In most cases the parts department is an entirely separate unit, but in small concerns the overall administration of the parts department could be part of the duties of a service manager. With the tremendous increase of vehicle population in recent years, the sale of parts has become a specialized and major part of service station business. All parts personnel need to be trained in Parts Merchandising and should take the C.G.L.I. course No. 381 (or 376) which covers this subject. Managers of such departments need to have the Advanced PARDIC certificate. The PARDIC certificate is issued by the Society of Motor Manufacturers and Traders upon satisfactory completion of a course of study and success in examinations dealing with parts merchandising. PARDIC is an acronym built up as follows: PARts/DIstribution Certificated training.

As with all other departments, the parts department must be well organized and efficient. The layout of a stores should be considered on—(a) its merchandising possibilities (b) the economic holding of stock (c) adequate area for stock and (d) future expansion, this latter item being very important bearing in mind that vehicle population is almost doubling every ten years.

A good and poor layout of a stores is shown in Figs 2.10 and 2.11. Access to all sections should be easy and time should not be wasted by having to wander round to poorly placed racks and bins. Bins should be arranged in symmetrical blocks and gangways. Lighting should be above storage racks and in the centre of gangways. Access to related departments such as the workshop and showrooms should be easy. Selling areas should be convenient for customers and be attractive to the public to induce them to come in and buy. Window space should not be blocked by racks and bins, thus obtaining good use of natural light.

The merchandising possibilities can be assessed by local vehicle population and volume of work normally taken into the workshop. Economic holding of stock is very important as all parts held in the stores means money standing idle. Parts department managers must obtain a turnover of all stock at least three times a year. Thus if a total of £210 000 turnover in stock is achieved each year, the actual holding of stock should be £210 000/3 = £70 000. Each

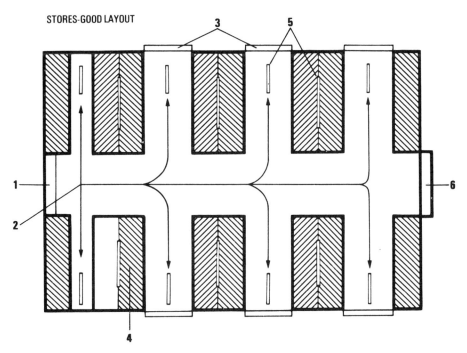

STORES-GOOD LAYOUT

1. Adequate serving counter
2. Clear gangway giving access to racks and bins
3. Unobscured windows making maximum use of natural light
4. Well-placed bins and racks in symmetrical order
5. Fluorescent strip lighting above racks and in the centre of gangways
6. Well-placed "goods inward" area with rack to hold parts awaiting storage in bins

Access to showroom, service and other departments should be good. Any office within a stores should give a clear view of most areas for the purpose of supervision

Fig. 2.10 Good Stores Layout

item in the stores will obviously sell at different rates, e.g. sparking plugs and replacement engines. However, by trying to have a 4 month stock or annual turnover of 3 times of all parts, we can assess how much stock to hold as follows:

1. Check last 3 months sales—say 80.

2. Deduct parts in stock—say 25,
$$80 - 25 = 55.$$

3. Deduct parts on order—say 10,
$$55 - 10 = 45.$$

4. Add customers pending orders—say 15,
multiply this by 2 = 30.

5. Add this figure to 45 to obtain the total order required to be sent to the manufacturer,
i.e. $30 + 45 = 75.$

STORES-POOR LAYOUT

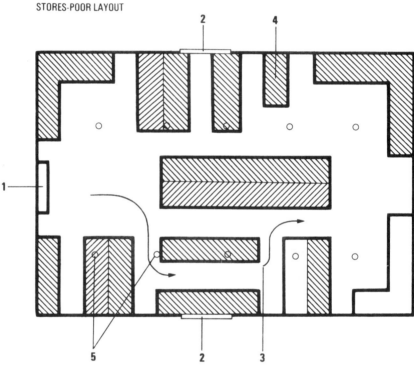

1. Serving counter and "goods inward" area causing confusion
2. Window space obscured-poor use of natural light
3. Devious, time consuming, path for assistants
4. Poorly-placed shelves at irregular intervals
5. Lighting placed in bad position

Fig. 2.11 Poor Stores Layout

No parts department can be expected to hold every part from the many thousands of parts that go to make up a modern motor vehicle. The department should, however, be capable of assessing the need for quickly-moving items and retain sufficient in stock by using a system similar to that indicated above. This system needs to be modified for seasonal changes, for example, anti-freeze solutions have a heavy demand in autumn but a light one in other periods. All departments should co-operate with the stores, for example car sales departments can mention accessories available in the stores to their customers and so on. Any window displays should *attract* attention by having a good central focal point which should *interest* a potential customer so that he has a *desire* to buy and will be able to take *action* by walking into the stores and purchasing the advertized item or items. Thus the principle of selling using the A.I.D.A. formula is followed. It is recommended that this principle should be used in all advertising including any circulars sent out by the garage.

Now all parts which are sold each and every day should be close to the selling area. In connection with stores an old but true statement is as follows: "Everytime a part is handled, something is added to its cost and nothing to its value'. Therefore, a little thought on binning of parts will achieve a lot less work with increased turnover. The binning of parts can be done by section order, i.e. engine parts, gearbox parts etc. or by part numbers. This latter method does help to locate parts quickly but runs into difficulty as part sizes vary so much. Consequently, some stores prefer the section method of handling parts, others use part number order.

Each bin will have its own stock card with a suitable method of recording 'in' and 'out' columns and give a balance. This should be completed by the store-man. Small items such as nuts and bolts will not be recorded as it takes too much time and is not worth the expense. The storeman must complete bin cards for all other stock. He should not issue any parts without a signed requisition and this should then be sent to the costing department. All references such as chassis number, engine number etc. should be quoted when ordering parts from a manufacturer and parts should be carefully recorded upon receipt any special orders being placed on one side for collection if necessary. As the storekeeper is responsible for all parts he should be reminded that losses will be his responsibility and no unauthorized persons are allowed in the stores. All except the largest items should be served through the hatch or over the counter. All ordered parts should be carefully recorded and followed up if not delivered by a particular time.

Keeping a check on stock is vital so that (a) obsolete stock is not held taking up vital space, (b) parts are being ordered as required to meet a turnover of 3 times a year, and (c) to ensure that pilfering is not taking place. Stock checks can be completed twice a year noting parts ordered, sold and in stock. A few bins can be checked each day making a perpetual stock check and thus not requiring an annual stock check. A bin card contains headings of Part No., Description of Part, Location of Part. Columns underneath this comprise Date, Receipt or Issue, In, Out, Balance. This type of card and a 'Stock Consumption Record Sheet' showing monthly sales of all parts, can be obtained from various suppliers of essential stores paper work.

Where a small stores is operated under the guidance of a service manager, stock control can be operated by having a Purchase Book and Issue Book to record receipts and issues. The Purchase Book will contain columns indicating date, description of part, quantity ordered, supplier, advice note number, trade cost, retail price, bin number. An issue book will contain columns to indicate date, description of part, quantity issued, retail price, bin number, job number and signature of person issuing the parts. Providing all parts ordered and issued are recorded this can be an effective method of stock control.

Work study

Throughout this book emphasis has been placed upon efficiency in all aspects of garage work. The use of work study methods is now applied in all industries and has been used in many garages for a long time. Work study methods are often applied without recognition as such. Take the apprentice mechanic who is trained to replace all tools clean and on the same position on the tool board. Supposing he leaves the tool dirty and in some obscure place: the next time he requires the tool, considerable time will be spent trying to find the tool. Thus, tidyness in a workshop is a form of training in work-study methods. The section of this book dealing with flow-lines is the application of time and motion study to the servicing of vehicles. Likewise standard repair schedules and standard times for services offered by manufacturers are all based on work study methods Good stores layouts with rapid turn-over items near to the serving hatch is yet another example of studying work and reducing time and effort to a minimum.

Work study is a subject which has many ramifications. The Institute of Work Study Practitioners has evolved many time saving methods by the scientific approach to job analysis. Correct use of principles can be applied to all aspects of work, and, if this results in a job being completed quicker with more bonus for employer and employee then this must be encouraged. The British Standards Institution detail important definitions in connection with this subject and the student would be well advised to study the appropriate sections as required. For example:

Method study. A study of the suitability of the tools or work aids and the manner in which they are employed.

Motion study. The study of the physical characteristics of the job requirements.

Motion economy. The analysis of motion study to minimize waste of human energy and to ensure a smooth and rythmic performance.

Time study. The measurement of the speed and effort required to produce a fair day's work.

Incentives. These are rewards designed to operate at a certain level of performance.

Work measurement. This is a modern derivation of Time Study.

Work study. Work study embraces Time Study and Motion Study and conditions which influence the job such as heat, fatigue, lighting etc.

By applying these it is possible to analyse a job in detail, and, where appropriate, to adjust the work routine so that the job is completed in less time or with less fatigue on the part of the operator. Manufacturers who issue standard service and repair job times carefully analyse all work required. For example if a replacement engine is required for a particular vehicle, the job itself will be timed by having a mechanic remove all necessary parts such as bonnet, radiator and hoses, carburettor and manifolds etc., and recording each operation on a Motion Analysis Sheet. The total time taken to complete the job is then obtained. A standard time achieved by having a number of operators complete the same job to obtain an average time. With due allowance being made for various conditions which can prevail the standard time becomes a time in which any skilled mechanic can easily complete the work set. In practice as referred to elsewhere dealing with bonus and incentive schemes, a skilled mechanic will save time and thus achieve his reward.

Work study can be applied to all jobs and if an assessment of time to be taken is required or if improvement of performance-is desired, then the procedure to adopt would be as follows:

1. Select the work to be studied or analysed.
2. Record all the facts about the work being done and the method being employed. This means recording times taken, where tools are taken from and replaced, physical movement of the operator i.e. where he walks, lifts and so on.
3. Examine all the facts critically and put in a written ordered sequence.
4. From the information gathered reorganize the work to develop the most practical economic and effective method to complete a job.
5. Make the new method a standard practice.
6. By regular checks make the standard practice routine by inspection at intervals to ensure the new method is being maintained.

This only outlines the basic ideas behind work study and further details can be obtained by consulting text books relative to this work. Even so, the good manager will know how to look at his general workshop organization bearing the above points in mind.

Workshop control systems and workshop loading

It is part of a manager's job to ensure that all his staff has a reasonable amount of work to do and to ensure that the staff complete their work. This does not mean that it is necessary to spy on mechanics who may have stopped to think about the job in hand. It is much better to approach a mechanic in a way that stresses that labour costs must be kept to a minimum rather than with an aggressive 'have you nothing to do?' Any experienced manager will know it is much better to make everyone feel part of the organization and to make everyone understand that wasted time does mean loss for the workshop and, as a result, loss of bonus for the staff.

A service station cannot be run on a hit or miss basis and work must be planned ahead and handled in a systematic manner if it is to function efficiently. Consequently, a service manager must organize his own routine in order that he can organize the work load of other staff. To do this he must list his own duties and how often these need attention.

Daily work

Check all staff present and work is distributed via foreman, deal with correspondence from customers, manufacturers, equipment suppliers. Deal with workshop and staff problems as they arise. Deal with warranty claims and complaints. Ensure training schemes are progressing satisfactory. Check invoices.

Weekly checks

a) *Inspection of premises* to see if any maintenance required e.g. windows broken, toilets clean and working, dirty workshop floor or corners require tidying, white parking lines need re-painting, lighting in good order, lifting equipment and tools satisfactory.

b) *Check all work received* (usually Monday or Tuesday) to see adequate work load for the shop staff and that all repairs and services are proceeding. Use magnetic colour blocks on cars so that a numerical sequence is obtained and any jobs held up can be easily spotted. Complete weekly Labour Analysis Charts.

Monthly checks

c) *Check profit and loss statement* covering repairs and service, the second week of the month is usually the best for this.

d) *Send out special service letters* reminding customers that their cars are due for service or offering some other service such as battery and lighting checks. Appraise current advertising and service promotion ideas.

e) *Take inventory of equipment* being used and check to ensure it is in good order or whether maintenance is required.

f) *Check decoration and painting of premises*—organize cleaning and decorating as required.

Twice monthly checks

g) *Check service follow-up* i.e. customers who have booked a service and failed to appear, likewise follow up truant customers for other work which may have been requested and customer has not turned up.

h) *Sales and works meeting* which can be held every second Tuesday or Wednesday but at a regular time to ensure work and departments are

co-operating and running smoothly. Iron out difficulties and disputes.
i) *Annual check*—check very carefully the annual financial report. Any parts not healthy should be considered carefully to see how these can be improved.

Bi-annual checks

j) *Check efficiency of all personnel.* How many staff require re-training or require to be placed on manufacturers' courses to be brought up-to-date? Arrange a rota for staff to go on such courses.
k) *Ensure all Factories Act reports for lifting equipment, compressors, boilers etc.* are filed and any repairs required put into effect.

These are the duties of a service manager. Such duties may be increased or decreased according to the size of the station. In any event a calendar showing these duties should be to hand to serve as a reminder to the manager and could be arranged as follows:

SUN	MON	TUES	WED	THUR	FRI	SAT
			1 h	2	3	4
5	6 a	7 b	8 g	9 c	10 e	11
12	13 a	14 b	15 h	16 f	17	18
19	20 a	21 b	22 g	23	24	25
26	27 a	28 b	29 h	30	31 d	

This calendar covers a monthly work programme which includes daily, weekly, monthly and bi-monthly checks.

The annual report for each firm should be studied when to hand and the yearly diary noted e.g. if the annual report becomes available each January then a date should be allocated to examine the report i.e. 25. Likewise the bi-annual checks should be appended in the diary calendar i.e. the dates these are to be carried out. Thus January 4th and July 4th could be appended as a reminder.

Some manufacturers such as Studebaker use a calendar with symbols such as circles, squares, triangles etc. to indicate job requirements, daily, weekly, monthly and annually.

In addition to these regular checks and inspections a service manager must also allocate time to recruit, interview, select, hire and dismiss personnel, complete R.T.I.T.B. claim forms, meet all vehicle purchasers, maintain good liason with other departmental managers, ensure good contact with insurance companies to maintain good volume of insurance work, supervise used car re-conditioning and new car preparation.

According to the size of station or dealership policy, these duties will be modified but the items listed gives some indication of the total responsibilities of a service manager.

Workshop loadings

Whilst the service manager may deal with workshop loadings the reception engineer will need to know when a job can be completed in the workshop. To load a shop with too much work means a customer is without his car for too long a period whilst too little work means mechanics stand idle. Thus a daily diary should be kept and full details noted of the customers name and address and the job required. If a repair job is needed the customer's car should be checked upon arrival and the job assessed e.g. a customer may assume a differential is at fault when the trouble may be caused by a wheel bearing. Normal servicing jobs are straight forward and time schedules from manufacturers are available. However, when keeping the diary the reception engineer should keep in very close liaison with the foreman to see how jobs are progressing and whether full staff is available or if any are off ill, going on courses and so on. Thus a reception engineer before accepting a job should bear in mind:

a) Number of mechanics in the shop i.e. 10 mechanics   8 hours = 80 hours per day working time (100% efficient—rarely achieved).

b) *Type of job* coming in (repair/service) and length of time required. Manufacturer's Standard Time Schedules for repair work should be consulted.

c) *Most convenient time* to accept job unless customer can leave a car all day. Rental costs for floor space should always be kept in mind.

d) *If parts are required* approximate length of time required to obtain these and whether they can be ordered before the job comes in: *liaison with store manager* is essential for this part of the work.

e) *Upon arrival of the job* a job card should be made out in duplicate, one for the office, one for the foreman to pass onto the mechanic unless a three or five part job set is used where one copy is the job card.

f) *Some form of indicator* should then be attached to the car to denote arrival time and date. Magnetic coloured holders in numerical order of jobs received are very useful and eye-catching, thus, blue for service work 1, 2, 3, 4 etc., red for repair work 1, 2, 3, 4 etc. When placed on top of a car these magnetic holders serve as a constant reminder that a job is held up for some reason. Colours can be changed daily if required.

The above points are relevant to workshop loading. Service schools in this country and in the U.S.A. stress these points and each have their own workshop loading sheets to keep control of jobs in hand and labour, for it must be remembered that profit on labour sales forms a vital part of every workshop.

The full utilization of labour can only be obtained by careful organization and planning which also has its limitations. No one can predict that a customer will not turn up or parts will be excessively delayed resulting in lost time but, all things being equal, the loading of a workshop can be controlled by using a Workshop Loading Chart. These charts which are usually about 50 centimetres (20 in) by 35 centimatres (14 in), are divided into columns to include Repair Order No., Customer's Name, Make and Model of Car, Registration No. of Car, details of Work to be Completed, Hours of Work expected, Collection Date and Time, Mechanic's Name, Name of Tester. A separate sheet is used for each day of each week. A customer telephoning for an appointment can be given a time and date by referring to the Workshop Loading Charts which are made out 7 to 10 days in advance, a new one being completed each day to include on it the day and date, all other details being already given.

In addition to control of labour and jobs in the workshop, the mechanic himself must be constantly reminded of his work load. A Daily Record Card of work done is one method of recording a mechanics' productive work. B.L.M.C. use the layout shown in Fig. 2.12. It will be observed that Schedule Time can be recorded either from a Manufacturers' Standard Time Schedule or by separate assessment by the reception engineer if such jobs are not given in the Manufacturers' Schedules. Thus, if a mechanic finishes the work before the stated time, he is credited with the stated time but can commence another job thus obtaining a bonus in 'time saved.' This card serves more than one purpose, not only recording a mechanics total time but also serving as a reminder to him of the work he has actually done. The foreman of the work-shop will keep these cards in a suitable tray and complete all recordings necessary. It is the foreman who gives out the work to the mechanics and he is able to keep a check on such allocation using his men to complete work in good time.

The service manager who has overall control of the workshop will receive the job cards from the foreman daily as jobs are completed. From the job cards he will transfer details of the mechanics attendance, overtime at $1\frac{1}{3}$ and $1\frac{1}{2}$ rates, schedule time for the job, non-productive time, internal time spent cleaning tools etc., and finally, assess each day by calculating time saved or lost. Obviously time saved is a vital part of the assessment and if a mechanic has a consistent run without time saved the service manager must determine why because 'time saved' means increased profit for the workshop. A Labour Sales Analysis Sheet on a weekly basis is arranged as shown in Fig. 2.13. In connection with 'time saved' and efficiency, the section of this chapter dealing with this should be consulted.

Service records and follow-up schemes

As indicated in the earlier part of this chapter, the hard copy of the 3 or 5 part job set is retained by the service manager for all repairs and services

DAILY RECORD CARD

NAME .... No. .... DATE ....

Job No.	Item No.	Item Comp	Sch Time	Productive Hrs.	Non Productive Hrs.		Clockings
						OFF	
						ON	
						OFF	
						ON	
						OFF	
						ON	
						OFF	
						ON	
						OFF	
						ON	
						OFF	
						ON	
						OFF	
						ON	
						OFF	
						ON	
						OFF	
						ON	
						OFF	
						ON	
						OFF	
						ON	
						OFF	
						ON	
						OFF	
						ON	

INCOMPLETED JOBS	C/F	A	B	C	ATTENDANCE	HRS. D
JOB No.	HRS.				(NORMAL) TIME	
		TIME SAVED = A − B			BONUS TIME	
		OVERTIME			ℓ 1.1/3	
					ℓ 1.1/2	

N.B.   D − C = B

Fig. 2.12 Mechanics' Daily Record Card

LABOUR SALES RECORD WEEK ENDING MONTH

COL. 1 = OPERATIVES ATTENDANCE HOURS. COL. 2 = CUSTOMER LABOUR STANDARD HOURS. COL. 3 = INTERNAL LABOUR HOURS. COL. 4 = NON-REVENUE LABOUR HOURS.

SHEET No.

SECTION	OPERATIVES NAME	No	Grade	DAY 1	2	3	4	DAY 1	2	3	4	DAY 1	2	3	4	DAY 1	2	3	4	DAY 1	2	3	4	DAY 1	2	3	4	OPERATIVES WEEKLY TOTALS 1	2	3	4	2 & 3 & 4	R.O.F.W. CORRECTED	O TIME	PAY HOURS	OPS No

TOTALS

EFFICIENCY %

Fig. 2.13 Labour Sales Analysis Sheet (Standard Triumph)

carried out. Keeping these enables a list of customers to be available if work appears to be slackening off, or upon referring to previous work records whether a slack period is anticipated for say, September or October. If this is the case a service manager can send out either service reminder letters or give a special offer of, for example, a braking system overhaul at a reduced price. With regular customers of course, service work can be anticipated. When one service has been done a record is kept in the form of a card diary indicating when the customer should be expected to call in say 3 or 6 months time. If the customer does not call then a reminder letter is sent out to him. Here are two examples:

Reminder for service

Dear Mr. . . . .

Upon referring to our records we note your car is now due for a further service. In case you have overlooked this rather important work, we are taking the liberty of reminding you.

If you would care to telephone or call we should be very pleased to arrange a suitable time and date for your car to receive attention.

Yours sincerely,

SERVICE MANAGER.

Work promotion letter to all past and present customers

Dear Customer,

During the next two weeks we are offering a complete diagnostic analysis of your car's condition for half the usual price!

Our trained technicians, using the latest diagnostic equipment will completely analyse the condition of your car and provide a detailed report. Any repairs which may be required could be carried out at our workshops or elsewhere: we would provide free estimates for such work.

Since we believe it to be in your interest to have your car checked at the reduced price we hope you will be able to call at our Service Department or telephone to arrange an appointment to suit you.

Yours sincerely,

SERVICE MANAGER.

Letters advertising other work might be written in a similar way.

Other service promotion schemes include advertising on local television, local cinema, local football team programmes, local press, posters, circulars,

G.P.O. 'yellow pages', signs at the station and roadside, window display and by distributing novelties such as key rings, calendars and so on.

At this point it would be as well to explain that service promotions fall into certain categories:

1. Continuous. Stamp trading comes within this group along with daily or weekly advertising.
2. Semi-continuous promotions usually last up to 20 weeks and embrace some form of 'collecting card' for the customer to complete and redeem the card for some specific item or discount on a car accessory of his own choice.
3. Short-term or 'instant' promotions are usually based on the purchase of a certain gallonage of petrol or oil. With purchase some special gift or discount is given for a limited period of time, e.g. 7 days, 14 days or 28 days only.

All promotions cost money and must be carefully chosen. At the close of any promotion its effect must be evaluated. For example the service manager must ask himself:

(a) What effect did the promotion have on sales?
(b) Did we take full advantage of the selling opportunities opened by the promotion?
(c) Did we achieve our original objectives—if not, why not?
(d) Was it worth the cost?
(e) Could a similar result have been obtained by a cheaper method?

The object of all promotions is to improve profitable sales and to enlarge the scope and prestige of the service station. Consequently when considering a sales promotion scheme the service manager must think well ahead to ensure he is going to market a saleable product at precisely the right time. The seasons of the year, holiday periods, etc., fall at regular intervals and provide a ready-made theme for many promotion activities. Nevertheless, the promotion must be well planned to have the maximum effect. By remembering at all times we are selling service, parts, accessories, new and used vehicles, etc., it is important to bear in mind that we must supply what the customer wants.

With any promotion the following items need to be considered:

1. The method of advertising, (i.e. local press, local television, leaflets, posters, circulars, etc.) is sufficient to achieve the desired object.
2. The cost of advertising will be justified by the increased profit obtained from the sales or services rendered.
3. Your staff are made aware of the promotion and will be able to handle the increased custom expected from the promotion scheme.
4. The promotion will meet the customer's needs at the time it is being offered.
5. Try to make your service station a place attractive enough to make the customer want to call again for service work, petrol or accessory sales.
6. Ensure your promotions are strictly honest and legal. Many motor traders

have been convicted in the courts because they have not paid sufficient attention to detail in wording their advertisements. The Trade Descriptions Act 1968 demands strict honesty. If a used car is advertised as 'immaculate' then that is just what it must be.

Warranty procedures and claims

To understand warranty procedures the structure of the retail trade should first be understood. A manufacturer is held responsible for the goods he sells but the retailer of the goods, in our case cars or commercial vehicles, is the person to whom defective goods are returned. The retailer then puts right jobs which the manufacturer authorizes and returns complete units where this is necessary. Therefore, the retailer has some claim on the manufacturer. The rate of reimbursement will be decided between manufacturer and distributor. All new vehicles are sent on order, from the manufacturer to a distributor who holds a franchise. A franchise is a privilege to distribute cars or commercial vehicles by one dealer in a certain area. Manufacturers appoint a distributor in a particular area and the number of distributors depends upon size and population of an area. One large manufacturer has 400 main distributors with a further 1 200 appointed dealers for car sales and 150 truck specialist distributors. The average number of employees for these establishments is 100, the highest being 250, the lowest 50. The larger dealerships can expect to sell some 2 000 cars/light vans a year. Distributors allow locally-appointed dealers to buy cars from them at a suitable discount. The line of distribution in the motor trade is therefore: manufacturer (producer)—wholesaler (distributor)—retailer (dealer)—consumer (customer).

In the event of a claim for defective work this line is reversed. The dealer makes out a Warranty Claim Form and sends this to the distributor who, in turn, sends this to the manufacturer. Sometimes a direct claim is possible from dealer to manufacturer. Also, distributors sell cars and commercials direct to customers as well as selling to dealers.

A Warranty Claim Form is shown in Fig. 2.14 and all details must be completed. Some manufacturers expect dealers and distributors to complete minimum warranty work of say, up to £2.00 for labour and materials. If this amount is exceeded then the Warranty Claim Form is made out and sent to the manufacturer's service department. This department besides being responsible for all claims also has to ensure that distributors and dealers 1) receive spare parts 2) receive technical information in the way of service manuals 3) organize refresher courses for mechanics belonging to dealers and distributors 4) provide special service tools as required; service manuals, parts catalogues along with modified sections are continuously sent to dealers from the manufacturer. A service manager should ensure these reach all people concerned by having each department sign on the front of the manual in turn. The manual is then filed in a central position for access as required by all personnel involved. A Warranty Clerk is sometimes appointed at service stations to deal exclusively

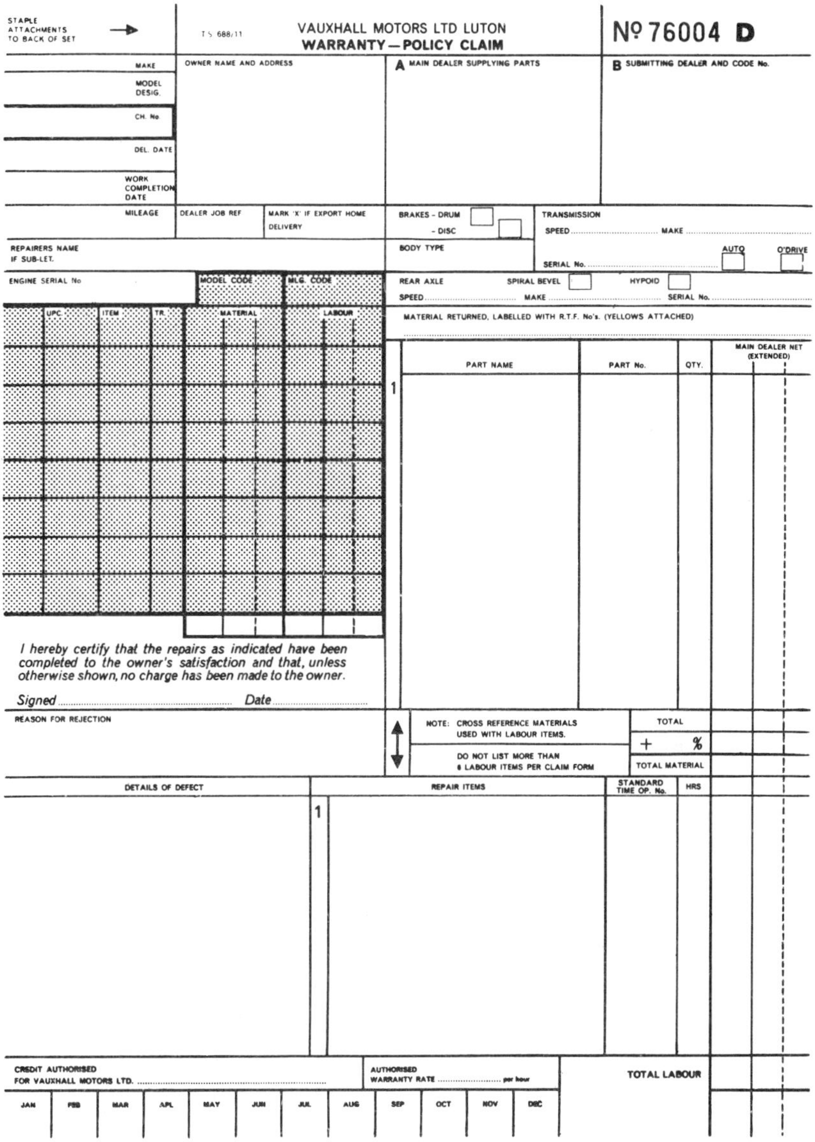

Fig. 2.14 Warranty Claim Form

with this work. This clerk must understand all warranty claims. Certain parts of a vehicle are guaranteed for different lengths of time, for example side and headlamp bulbs for 28 days, radio parts for 3 months and so on. Details of such guarantees are supplied by the manufacturer.

A transport fleet operator who has a number of cars or trucks is usually entitled to special discounts, for example $2\frac{1}{2}\%$ with eleven vehicles or more and 10% on 200 or more vehicles. Percentages will vary between the figures quoted depending on the number of vehicles and these are called 'fleet users terms.' These discounts offer advantages to manufacturer and customer as well as to the dealer who sells and will probably service and repair the vehicles.

Having read this chapter which deals with administration details, students are advised to consult their own employers to ascertain how their systems operate. In addition, colleges who run management courses will generally arrange visits to large efficient dealerships. Students during such visits would complete the answers, on separate sheets, to a questionnaire similar to that shown below. By this method a student is able to see how theory is put into practice.

Visit to a main dealership—questionnaire

1. What system is employed at reception when a customer arrives with his car?
2. How is workshop loading controlled?
3. If there is a bonus scheme in operation—how does it operate?
4. Outline the flow of job cards in this dealership.
5. What items make up a Profit and Loss Account for the workshop?
6. How are overheads allocated to the workshop?
7. Briefly state the turnover of stock in the stores and how stock checks are made.
8. Sketch to scale, a plan of the workshop area and indicate the position of all major items of equipment, viz., benches, lifts, pits, brake tester, chassis dynamometer, steering equipment, engine analysers and so on.

Questions

1. Describe the best methods of Part Stock Control and Ordering which you know, and which can be applied to a Dealers Part Store to ensure adequate but not excessive stocks at all times. (I.M.I.)
2. A Repair Order Card is a most important document. What information should it give and what procedure should it follow from the time it is completed until the Invoice is made out? (I.M.I.)
3. Modern cars are being designed for much less frequent maintenance periods. This will mean that customers will call at their service stations at larger intervals. Is it considered wise to operate a 'Customer Follow' system under these circumstances and what is the best system you know? (I.M.I.)

4. As a service manager with the stores under your control, what system would you adopt to see that you do not run out of any particular parts? How would you prevent obsolete stock choking your shelves? (I.M.I.)

5. If a service station, during a month, purchases x number of hours from its mechanics, and sells the same number of hours to its customers is said to be 100% efficient. This is a state of affairs rarely, if ever, achieved. What is considered to be a satisfactory percentage of efficiency in a service station, and what steps should be taken to achieve this figure assuming the department was not reaching it? (I.M.I.)

6. State how to assess an hourly rate of charge for work to include not only direct labour charges but also all consumable and processing materials used in a Body Repair Section of a service station. (I.M.I.)

7. Make out a specimen requisition docket for the spares necessary to reline the brakes of a car and decarbonize its engine. Give your reasons for the layout of the form used. (I.M.I.)

8. With labour and other costs continually rising it is essential to ensure that the Workshop or service station is kept as fully employed as possible. Describe any system which you consider is best to fulfill the above requirement. State the number of employees on which your answer is based. (I.M.I.)

9. It has often been said that 'Sales follow Service.' If it were necessary for you to organize an Advertising Campaign to sell Service, how would you do it and how would you evaluate the results compared with the costs of the campaign? (I.M.I.)

10. Imagine you have taken over a workshop with twenty skilled mechanics and, of course, the other workshop personnel. The parts department attached serves both your workshop and over the counter sales, but has not kept up with the growth rate for the area it serves and requires complete reorganization. How would you carry out the necessary reorganization? (I.M.I.)

11. Most dealerships comprise three main departments, viz., sales, service and spares. Each must make its contribution to the profits of the company. As the person in charge of service, what system would you use to make sure that your department was making a profit, or a loss? This is assuming that the overheads allocated to each department are known by the head of the department. (I.M.I.)

12. An inventory of a Parts Department has disclosed a high percentage of slow moving and obsolete material in stock. Suggest how to clear this material and to ensure that in the future this position could not be repeated. (I.M.I.)

13. The way a Warranty or Guarantee Claim is handled can either cement or destroy customer goodwill. Describe how you would handle a major claim from the time the complaint is received to final settlement. (I.M.I.)

14. Much valuable workshop space is often taken up by vehicles waiting for spare parts. In many cases this should not have been necessary. How would

you organize your parts stock and your Reception/Workshop/Parts department relations in order to cut this waste to the absolute minimum? (I.M.I.)

15. With costs rising everywhere it is most essential that proper records are kept in order to balance revenue received for Service against the cost of operating the service station. How would you record the production of your mechanics both individually and collectively. (I.M.I.)

16. Your Parts department has a turnover of £50 000 per year, serving both your workshop and the public:

    (1) What should the value of your stock holding be?

    (2) How would you control the stock in order to maintain and probably increase your sales turnover?

    (3) How would you control the issue of parts to your workshop?

    (I.M.I.)

17. Paperwork in a garage is essential for the control of costs. Explain the object of 3 and 5 part job sets which are now used in modern workshops. State what each copy will be used for and where each copy is finally retained. (I.M.I.)

18. Speedy invoicing is essential. State why this is so and the object of obtaining a customers signature for work to be carried out. (I.M.I.)

19. What are Fleet User Terms, to what do they apply, and who is entitled to them? (I.M.I.)

20. Vehicle manufacturers regularly send out Service Information which usually goes to the service manager. Some items are of such a nature that certain members of Sales and Spares departments should know of them. How would you ensure that not only the members of the Service department but also those concerned in the other two departments know of them? (I.M.I.)

21. The time spent by skilled mechanics at the Parts Counter still appears to be too high in some repair shops. Describe any system that you know which will eliminate this waste of highly-skilled men's time, or at least reduce it to a minimum. (I.M.I.)

CHAPTER 3

RECEPTION

Reception engineers (service advisers)

Qualifications and responsibilities

The 'reception engineer' also known as 'service adviser' or 'receptionist', is a most important part of any service station. It is the reception engineer who meets the customer and finally hands back a car when a service or repair has been completed. Consequently, the behaviour and attitude of a reception engineer can reflect an image of a service station to a customer. If this image is poor then it is unlikely a customer will return. On the other hand, a reception engineer who instills confidence into a customer and is pleasing in attitude and appearance will inevitably find such customers returning for further service and repair work. Too often the general public complain—and quite rightly in many cases—that a garage was completely indifferent to a genuine complaint about a new car or about work which has been completed and is incorrect. It would appear to the general public that some service stations are disinterested about their custom. This, of course, is a disastrous state of affairs and can only result in poor profits for the organization as a whole. The reception engineer, then, plays a vital role in attracting customers and keeping them. To do this job he must have certain qualities and the qualifications for the job could be outlined as follows:

1) Good practical background, e.g., a fully-trained mechanic or fitter.
2) Good theoretical background such as indicated by a pass in final C.G.L.I. 375 Motor Vehicle Mechanics' work or, preferably, C.G.L.I. 390, Motor Vehicle Technicians' work.
3) In addition to good practical and theoretical knowledge so that he can converse on all aspects of repair work with confidence, a reception engineer must have a pleasing personality. He must be pleasant at all times with customers, dress smartly, have a clean appearance and be able to instil confidence into customers about the work the garage will do.

Responsibilities of a reception engineer

It has already been stated what the general background of a reception engineer should be. The responsibilities of a reception engineer can be outlined as follows:

1) To meet the customer before and after repair or service work. When meeting the customer he must carefully assess the fault with the car. To do this, he can complete a road test with the car with the customer driving or use equipment which may be available for such work. In any event, the reception engineer will a) decide upon the work to be done b) obtain customer approval for such work c) place an immediate order for parts with the Parts department if required.

2) The reception engineer having obtained approval for repair, will then make out an estimate for the work or will complete a 3 part or 5 part job card set. (These are dealt with in Chapter 2 in detail.) Such estimates or job sets are then sent to the service manager for his approval.

3) Part of the 3 or 5 part job set is a job card for the mechanic. If this system is not used a job card must be made out and passed to the workshop foreman.

4) A record of workshop loading must be kept at reception to ensure that a car or commercial vehicle can be taken at a certain time and date. This must be checked carefully with the workshop foreman each and every day as mechanics can fail to turn up for work because of illness and for other domestic reasons.

5) Depending on the system of costing adapted, it may be necessary for the reception engineer to prepare the invoice or bill for forwarding to the accounts department of the garage. The 3 and 5 part job set uses one of the sheets as an invoice and this then passed to the accounts department.

6) Finally, the reception engineer must hand the car back to the customer, receive payment if an account is not open with the garage and send the customer on his way—content with the repair and the bill for the job. From the customer's point of view he needs to feel he has had a) cheerful reception b) full attention to his instructions c) rapid and accurate service d) reasonable and consistent charges with the bill presented at the proper time i.e. when taking the car away from the workshop or at the end of the month e) that the garage has been honest with all aspects of work completed.

These are the general responsibilities of a reception engineer but there is far more involved in these responsibilities than meets the eye! Complaints do occur even with the best of garages but these can be minimized by careful inspection of work after service or repair. In the connection a reception engineer has not only an obligation to the customer to listen but must also bear in mind his obligations to the car manufacturer and his own employer. Some customers, for example, expect free repairs long after the warranty of a car expires simply because they have only completed a very low mileage. This does involve the handling of complaints which we shall deal with later, in the meantime let us see how many complaints can be avoided by a careful inspection procedure following repair, service or delivery of a new car.

Quality control of workshop repairs, service or sale of new and used cars

It is a distressing thought that many service stations have virtually no inspection of work done and are quite happy to have a high return of cars for correction of faulty work. The worst of these expect 50% of cars serviced, repaired, or a sale of a car, to return for work to be done. Many have a 20% return of work whilst an average is 10%. The aim should be no return of work but accepting only 2%! No matter how this return of work is viewed it still results in mechanics, receptionists and other members of staff having to repeat, for nothing, certain jobs to put the car right. No efficient garage can tolerate such a loss of profits nor the upsetting of a customer who expects good quality work. It is appreciated there always will be human error but so many defects could be corrected before the vehicle leaves the workshop saving time, money and customer dissatisfaction. This can be achieved by checking all work done in the workshops by the mechanics. Whilst a 'tester' is employed in some workshops this work often falls to the reception engineer.

Function of an inspection system

Applied to our trade this could be defined as the means by which a repair or service is checked and certain standards achieved. Inspection is a preventative measure as it seeks to prevent defective work either arising or being allowed to proceed, thus, only acceptable work goes forward either as a new or used car, or as a satisfactory repair. Mechanics commence such inspections for, as skilled men they should be able to execute skilled work without supervision and it should be satisfactory.

However, assuming we are going to quality control all work, the reception engineer or tester must satisfy himself that a car is, as far as can be ascertained, in good order. A road test of 5 miles can normally reveal defects and for certain work is still essential e.g. steering or suspension where equipment is not available to dynamically check such work. Full use of electronic engine tester, 'rolling road', brake tester should be made as these are valuable aids to quality control most types of work. A three or five minute test run on the chassis dynamometer is time well spent if a car does not come back for further attention. Certain chassis dynamometers and brake testers give graphical recordings, thus, a customer can have both before and after results if desired.

From this it will be seen that an area for quality control of all work must be set on one side of all workshops. This is shown in one layout in Chapter 1. From what has been written, to quality control work, the following procedures could be adopted.

Service work

a) Check type of service i.e. 3 000, 6 000, 12 000, etc.
b) An assessment of performance can be made using diagnostic centre or road test. Electronic equipment will reveal work not done—dirty plugs, points incorrectly set etc.
c) Ensure no oil or grease is on the steering wheel, pedals or exterior of the car.

Repair work

a) Check nature of repair e.g. brakes, transmission etc.
b) Complete test for repair only but note any other defects which may be revealed. Test on brakes could be on brake tester and recorded if possible. Whatever repair is completed, it should be checked to ensure it is satisfactory. If not return to mechanic for correction.
c) Ensure car is clean as before.

Sale of new and used cars

Pre-delivery inspection of the car is essential. In addition to mechanical aspects of the car, bodywork, upholstery, door locks, in fact all the car should be completely checked by using a special inspection sheet. Manufacturers of cars rely upon dealers to pick up any minor defects and correct them before a car is delivered. New cars are usually waxed and dewaxing forms part of the pre-delivery work. One of the biggest complaints of customers lies with defects on new cars and this reflects on the manufacturer and the service station who supplies the car. Vehicle salesmen should be trained and educated to meet R.T.I.T.B. requirements and take C.G.L.I. course number 382.

Handling complaints

We have seen that human error will, from time to time, result in a job being returned in spite of an effective inspection system. New parts, which have formed part of a repair will sometimes fail after test and so a customer returns with his car. It can be most annoying to anyone who takes a car from a workshop only to find that the repair fails after a low mileage. Furthermore it can involve considerable expense, for example, a capacitor failure on a motorway or no oil in a repaired rear axle seizing up on a motorway, will involve an expensive tow and could result in a claim against the garage which repaired the car. Hence the need for the quality control of jobs already mentioned. However, the fact remains that the customer will return and the reception engineer will have to deal with him or her. First, the reception engineer must listen to the nature of the complaint and determine that it is a faulty repair, service or broken part for which the garage could be held responsible. In the case of new cars, this would be dealt with under warranty and details are given in Chapter 2. With defective service, for example contact breaker points not set correctly resulting in power loss, then the reception engineer will have to use his judgement to see if this is a bona fide case. Customers have been known to alter adjustments, find such re-adjustments result in poor performance and then are unable to correct such work. It is true to say this applies to a very small minority of customers and, consequently, the reception engineer should show a genuine interest in such complaints. Furthermore, such complaints should receive immediate attention and be promptly rectified. A customer would accept that an error could arise but it should always be stressed that inspection of all cars is made. An apology for inconvenience never goes astray and providing the customer is made to feel his complaint has been handled with courtesy and has received attention he will be pleased to return to the workshop again. No customer should be kept waiting because it is 'a complaint' only as this can antagonize anyone. 'The customer is always right' is an old maxim but a valuable one.

Inevitably, the odd customer will return and swear something has gone wrong following a repair which has had no bearing on it whatsoever. Here, the invoice, which has detailed the exact repair is a vital aid on the part of the service station. The need for correct invoicing is essential and is stressed in Chapter 2. However, if we assume a customer has had a new clutch and 4 weeks later a universal joint becomes defective, he may fully expect rectification free of charge as he might not realize that two entirely different jobs are involved. This is where the invoice and the reception engineer's necessary qualifications are used to his and the garage's benefit. He must tactfully but firmly explain the position without insulting the customer. The service manager can always assist if required or asked for his opinion by the customer.

Service and sales

The selling of used cars is normally one of the functions of a dealership. Used cars always need attention of some kind and, the car sales department will call upon the workshop to execute the repairs needed. The *car sales* allow for repairs in part exchange allowances and the cost of such repairs must be paid for by the car sales department. In making a profit and loss account for each department a workshop must pay its way and make a profit. All departments **must** do the same. Thus, when a car comes into the workshop for complete renovation each job must be carefully estimated and costed as if it was a customer's car in for repair. The car sales department will then pay the cost of such repairs and the workshop will be credited with the repair work. Cases have arisen where a car sales department of a garage have found their own workshop prices far too high and they have had work done outside their own organization: an incredible situation! Obviously something is wrong since car sales departments and the workshop must work together to get the maximum gain from all trading of cars. Some unimportant jobs could be left— for example a small upholstery tear—depending just how old the car is and its cost. No car can be allowed to be sold which is unsafe in any way. By liaison with the car sales, precise repair bills can be agreed upon and, where necessary, a warranty for a used car given. Here, use of the quality control bay will be essential so that car sales do not get a bad name, nor, in turn, the workshop.

Service can be sold with a car and in this way help not only car sales department but the repair shop also if such work is costed correctly. A *free* service of a new or used car can help each department to support one another. In advertising new and used cars, special services can also be sold to the public. *Service Weeks* have been advertised and operated successfully. Such weeks are used to offer a service at a reduced price to attract custom, similarly car sales might offer *special reductions*. These *weeks* are organized when business is likely to be slack to help keep all staff fully employed. It is, of course, always possible to become so deluged with work as a result that it becomes impossible to cope and thus a certain disadvantage is developed by not being able to live up to what is advertised. On the other hand such arrangements can attract new business and staff could be requested to work overtime prior to the week in question so that all work could be completed in time.

Questions

1. A dealer organization comprises a sales, parts, service and accounts department each being to a large degree dependent upon the other. Describe briefly how the service department can help each of these, and what assistance they can expect in return. (I.M.I.)
2. Complaints of inefficiency are sometimes made against repair shops because of lack of co-operation between customer, receptionist, mechanic and tester. How would you ensure that such complaints were reduced to a minimum? (I.M.I.)
3. A customer of some years standing with a certain service station, demands that the necessary repairs and adjustments to his car be completed by a certain mechanic. How should a service manager, faced with this problem, reply to that customer's demands? If unable to agree, what reasons should be given? (I.M.I.)
4. With operating costs continually rising, discuss whether servicing costs could be reduced without reducing the standard of workmanship and without reducing wages. (I.M.I.)
5. Describe a system of inspection to ensure the highest possible standard of work being maintained in a service department. (I.M.I.)
6. There are many ways in which a service department may charge the sales department for work done. Which system do you prefer and why? (I.M.I.)
7. With most mechanics to-day working on an Incentive Bonus scheme, it is more essential than ever to see that only the best quality work leaves your workshop. What system would you employ to see that faulty work was reduced to the absolute minimum? (I.M.I.)
8. It is common practice to hold service weeks:
   (a) What are the objects of such weeks?

(b) How and when would you organize one?

(c) What are the advantages or disadvantages of them? (I.M.I.)

9. In order to operate a workshop successfully the amount Rectification of Faulty Work must be kept down to an absolute minimum. How would you achieve this object in a workshop under your control? (I.M.I.)

10. Explain how you would deal with the following situation:
Your workshop has appraised a used vehicle for the sales department and said the vehicle wants x pounds spent on it. The sales department complete the sale, then come back to you and say the deal was so tight that they can only afford to spend half the amount you have quoted. (I.M.I.)

11. As it is most important to recruit the right personnel for staff positions such as reception engineers or shop foremen, state what characteristics you would look for and what questions you would ask when interviewing an applicant for either of the two posts mentioned. (I.M.I.)

12. A customer's reaction to a service station is mainly based on the quality of work carried out on his car. State the supervision and inspection necessary to ensure satisfactory results in this direction. (I.M.I.)

CHAPTER 4

COLLISION REPAIR

Accident repair work

One of the greatest tragedies associated with the motor vehicle retail and repair trades is the terrible accident rate involving motor vehicles. In 1958, 237 265 vehicles were in collision on roads in the United Kingdom. The number of collisions in 1968 had increased to 291 275 and in a further 10 years the total collisions is expected to be close to 350 000. The loss of life and limb is a tragedy in itself and the material loss in damage amounts to millions of pounds. Repairing the damaged vehicles forms a vital part of the profits for a lot of garages but, like all other aspects of repair work, it must be done efficiently to obtain maximum profits.

Most collision damage is covered by insurance. All vehicles must have a minimum of third party cover whilst a large amount of vehicles have fully comprehensive insurance cover. This means that work coming into a body repair shop is paid for either by the customer direct or by an insurance company. Consequently, when a vehicle arrives for repair work, the first thing a workshop manager must do is to determine who is going to pay the bill. If a customer is to pay the bill then an estimate is prepared for the customer but we will consider this later.

Where a vehicle is involved in a collision the insured, that is the customer, will make out an accident claim form obtained from his insurance company. This will detail the nature of the accident and where the vehicle has been taken for repair. Some companies authorize work to proceed immediately but in any case body repairers usually prefer to have their work authorized in writing before commencing any work on the damaged vehicle. This is the best method to adopt from the body repairers view as it does eliminate any argument.

Assuming the repair is to be covered by insurance then the first stage of the repair work is to make out an estimate for the damage and then to contact the insurance company so that their assessor, or engineer as he is also called, can visit the workshop to examine the damaged vehicle and consider the estimate. A typical form of estimate is shown in Fig. 4.1. The actual number of copies of the estimate to be prepared will depend upon the system adopted by the

ESTIMATE

No. ....

CHARLES H. ALLEN (BODIES) LTD.

Works :
JUTSUMS LANE,
ROMFORD. ESSEX.

Registered Office
17 LONDON ROAD · ROMFORD · ESSEX

Telephones : ROMFORD 45091 (8 Lines)

Mr. R. Smith
200, Victor Avenue,
BARKING. ESSEX.

Telegrams : "MOTORS, ROMFORD."

DATE

Vehicle:	FORD CORTINA MK 11		Mileage:	46362
Chassis No.: BA 98GE 12345	Reg. No.:	ABC 123 A	Policy No.:	

Remove frontbumper, bumper irons, headlamps,
front flasher lamps, grille, bonnet, radiator.
O/side front door, horns and battery.
Cut away O/Side fender, bonnet closure panel.
front lower apron panel, and O/side headlamp
panel.
Reshape O/Side engine valence N/Side fender and
O/side radiator mounting panel.
Weld in and metal finish new O/Side fender, bonnet
closure panel, front lower apron panel, O/side
headlamp panel and front body re-inforcement panel
Re-hang O/side front door and new bonnet panel,
adjust clearances and seal all joints.
Re-paint front end of vehicle from door to door,
re-assemble vehicle replacing listed parts.

LABOUR 75 | 75

Supply
PARTS TO BE CHARGED AT MANUFACTURERS CURRENT
LIST PRICE

Bonnet.
Bonnet moulding
Front bumper (exchange)
Grille.
O/side headlamp bezel
N/S headlamp bezel
P/side flasher lamps
Front lower apron panel
Bonnet closure panel
O/side fender
O/Side headlamp panel.
Front body re-inforcement panel assy.
Radiator bottom hose.

Plus
Sundries as required.

Customers' cars are only driven by our staff at
customers' own risk and responsibility

Fig. 4.1 Estimate of Repair Work

workshop manager. For example some workshops find it convenient to type out six copies and these are distributed as follows: 1) stores for ordering spares as required, 2) workshop for full details of job to be done, 3) costing for accurate assessment of the final bill, 4) office for retention by the workshop manager to enable him to keep a check on the job, 5) assessor for his retention, 6) spare copy for customer or assessor if required. Needless to say, the number of copies can be reduced if the organization is small, For example, costing and office copies could be both completed or used as one. Likewise the stores and workshop copies could be completed together. Nevertheless, for the price of copies of the estimate, each section having individual copies can avoid hold up of work and allows paper-work to flow smoothly.

On the estimate it will be observed that the present method is to include labour prices which are current at the time. Parts' prices change from week to week and insurance companies are quite prepared to accept the current prices as per manufacturers' catalogue when the work is completed.

To prepare the estimate a detailed knowledge of body repair work is essential. This knowledge can only come through an apprenticeship in the trade. Thus, an estimator in a body repair shop will have served his apprenticeship in the trade and will have an appropriate City and Guilds of London Institute certificate such as 385 course or 378 Vehicle Body Work Courses or similar qualifications such as Part B section of I.M.I. examinations dealing with body construction and repair.

However, having made out the estimate form, the insurance assessor will now visit the workshop and approve or amend the work to be done. Insurance companies are not charity organizations and they will only want to pay for the accident damage and not other body work requiring attention because of rusting and so on. The insurance assessor is usually a trained and qualified engineer and will know exactly what is a fair price for the actual collision repair. On visiting the repair firm the assessor will verify repairs required and at the same time state if the customer is liable for the first £10, £20, £50 and so on. These are known as policy excess payments also referred to as endorsements for policies. In any event, where these exist, the customer will have to pay this amount and the workshop manager will get approval and a signature from the customer to proceed with the work. In a similar manner approval will also be obtained from the insurance assessor. It cannot be stressed too strongly that all estimates should detail all the work required. A very careful examination of the vehicle should be made to ensure that nothing is omitted.

At this point it is as well to mention that insurance companies have endorsements and condition clauses written into some of their motor insurance policies. For example, a spares endorsement could indicate that the company would be liable to replace the cost of a part as stated in the manufacturers' catalogue. Whilst this may be obvious and fair, cases have arisen where parts were not available and a new part has to be made at many times the cost of a part from the manufacturers. Such cases arise with old vehicles or vehicles made abroad where shipment of parts creates difficulties. In a similar way, the insurance company which writes into its policies 'the car can be removed to the repairers and instructions given for reasonable and necessary repairs to be commenced subject to a detailed estimate being obtained as soon as possible and sent forthwith to the Company' is operating a conditional clause.

Having obtained approval all round, the repair work can now proceed.

A good body repair shop needs to have highly-skilled workmen and good tools for body-repair work. Workshop equipment is mentioned in Chapter 1 but for a body repair shop the essential equipment could be listed as follows:

1. A well planned layout operating on a flow line principle if possible. Whilst each and every repair presents individual difficulties it is possible to have repairs organized so that major work is completed in one area, minor work in another, sanding and flatting in another and finally painting.
2. Alignment jigs for body and chassis checks.
3. Portable sanders. Air-operated sanders are preferred for safety, finish and as a means of deterring theft of the tools (air-operated tools are useless unless a good air supply is available).
4. Pullers and Dozers to pull out or push in damaged sections.
5. Sheet-metal cutting and forming tools such as guillotines, folders, light presses, air-operated chisels.
6. Comprehensive panel beating tools viz. dollies, spoons, hammers etc.
7. Welding equipment to include oxyacetylene, metallic-arc, resistance welding machines (spot welders) and/or CO_2 welding machines.
8. A well planned spray booth adjacent to a suitable hot-bake oven for drying purposes.
9. Fire-fighting equipment.

As stated in Chapter 1, a list of suppliers of equipment can be found in trade journals but much valuable information in connection with bodywork equipment will be obtained from S.A.B.R.E. Information Office, 190 Castelnau, London, S.W. 13.

Safety in or near any paint spraying operations is vital. Strict observation of No Smoking signs, clean floor, use of masks, fire extinguishers prominently displayed and always ready for use, should be enforced.

The Completion Note

Having gone through the repair shop, the finished vehicle is brought back for the customer to collect. The customer will inspect the work and if satisfied will sign a completion note, (sometimes referred to as a Satisfaction Note), stating the work has been done satisfactorily. The completion note is part of every accident insurance repair job and is required by the insurance company so that a client is unlikely to come back several months later complaining that something was not done or something else has arisen as the result of the previous accident. Consequently, it is the responsibility of the customer to indicate satisfaction. This does not mean a customer cannot return with defective paintwork or other faulty work which has been done as part of the repair. Most body repair shops would always correct such faulty workmanship but would not be prepared to do work not connected with the original estimate. It is in everyones interest that the completion note is signed by the customer and the vehicle should not be allowed out of the workshop until a signature is obtained.

This outlines the operation of a body repair workshop. As recommended in other chapters, a visit organized by a college (by arrangement with the proprietors) to a well-organized and equipped body repair workshop would prove to be a valuable aid to all students. A typical questionnaire to be answered during the visit might be as follows:

1. When a damaged vehicle comes to the workshop who makes out an estimate and what does this involve?
2. When an accident to a car is covered by insurance what must the manager of the workshop do before commencing work?
3. Explain the importance of a conditional clause and spares endorsement in a policy and explain how these can affect this workshop.
4. Sketch to scale a layout of the repair workshop and show where all major items are located, e.g. paint booth, alignment jigs, welding equipment, finishing equipment, quality control.
5. Make a line diagram of the flow of a job through this workshop.
6. State all the methods of welding employed and explain which jobs each method is suitable for giving a clear example.
7. Itemize all safety precautions enforced in the workshop.
8. Before a vehicle leaves the workshop a completion note is signed by the customer. Who obtains this signature and why is it important? Has a customer any redress once the note has been signed?

Questions

1. Give a brief description of how you would handle an accident repair from the time you receive the vehicle into your workshop to handing back to the customer, with particular attention to the co-ordination by all sections concerned. (I.M.I.)
2. When properly controlled, accident repairs are a very profitable source of revenue. Describe the procedure to ensure the preparation of an estimate for repairs and the processing of the repair through its various stages. (I.M.I.)
3. As a service manager, you are proposing to set up a body repair section and also a paint shop. Describe what equipment you would require and what safety precautions must be maintained in each section. (I.M.I.)
4. Insurance repairs has been the subject of some criticism recently for length of time from accident to completion, and from a cost angle. Explain how you would deal with such a repair bearing both the above points in mind. (I.M.I.)

5. In connection with insurance repairs explain the following terms and give an example of the application of each term:
   (a) Completion note
   (b) Conditional clause
   (c) Endorsement
   (d) Excess payment. (I.M.I.)

CHAPTER 5

STAFFING

Staffing a service station

A service station needs a wide variety of staff with varying degrees of skill and knowledge. As the size of service stations vary considerably, the type and number of staff will differ to meet the requirements of individual stations. From the very small garages employing 6 to 10 staff, we have large organizations employing up to 300 personnel. Future garages will have to be fairly big in order to justify the investment of capital for equipment needed to service modern cars and commercial vehicles; the staff required will also be large in number.

The staff required to operate a service station will normally consist of the following:
Directors including managing director, service manager, parts department manager, car sales manager, forecourt manager, receptionists (service advisers), workshop foreman, chargehands, mechanics, semi-skilled mechanics, apprentices, office staff, cleaners, labourers.

This is a general layout and their order within the structure of a garage is shown in Fig. 5.1. A variation of a staff layout is shown in Fig. 5.2.

Each member of staff shown in the organization chart will require to have a certain knowledge and skill. Perhaps the most important of all selection commences with apprentices, for here a considerable amount of time and money is invested in the hope that ayoung man will eventually become a skilled mechanic, technician engineer, body builder/repairer etc. It is, therefore, vital that wastage be avoided by using some means of selection. Ideally, every apprentice coming into the trade should have received a good basic education with four or five G.C.E. 'O' levels (or C.S.E.) with mathematics, science, technical drawing, English and metalwork amongst the subjects passed. If a prospective apprentice has these 'O' levels or C.S.E. passes, he is well on the way to proving his suitability for an apprenticeship. Academic attainment, however, is only part of the requirements of an apprentice, as we shall see later on in this chapter, but before we consider these other attributes, let us consider the young enthusiastic boy approaching a service manager for an apprenticeship when the boy has no 'O' levels at all. Should he be turned down

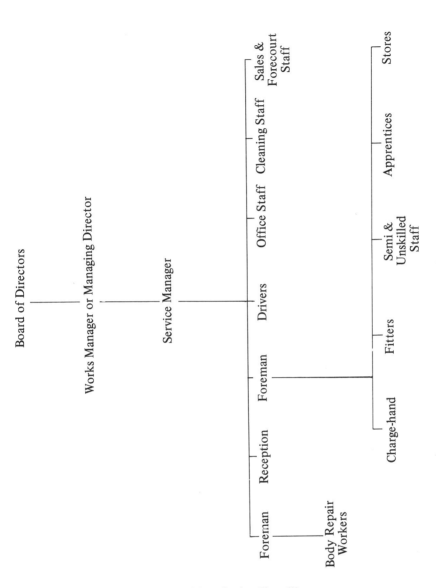

Fig. 5.1 Staff Organization Chart (1)

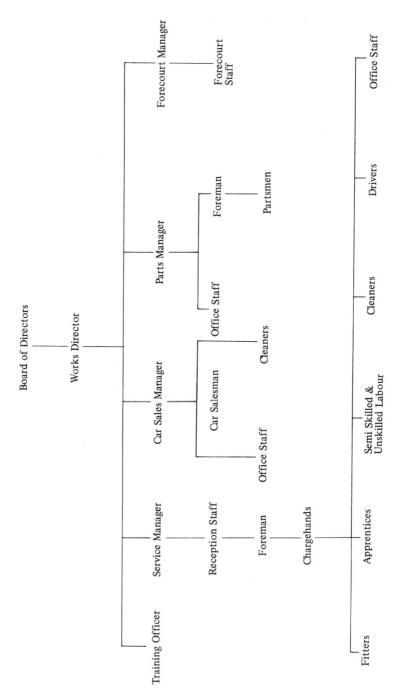

Fig. 5.2 Staff Organization Chart (2)

without consideration? Is it fair for a service manager to appoint or reject an applicant for an apprenticeship because the manager likes the look of a boy or, conversely, he doesn't look the right type? This haphazard method of choice sometimes does work, but it can be unfair and unjust to both employer and employee. Before a boy commences any apprenticeship he must have a reasonable intelligence in order that he can absorb the wealth of detailed knowledge required by all skilled personnel in the motor vehicle trades. If a boy does not have the necessary intelligence, it is surely unfair to ask him to try to do something beyond his capabilities. So how can we assess an eager young man who could prove to be a good tradesman even though he may not possess 'O' levels or equivalent C.S.E. passes?

Many service managers make full use of local technical colleges where trained lecturers can give selection tests to determine the suitability of a boy for a particular motor vehicle trade. Some garages employ a training officer to administer such tests, but, because of the specialized nature of such selective tests, most garages will request the assistance of local technical colleges.

Academically, a boy must have a reasonable attainment in arithmetic and certainly must have mechanical comprehension of a good level if he is to have the basic requirements of a good mechanic or fitter. It is possible that a boy may have disliked school simply because he was not allowed to apply his knowledge to practical matters that held his interest such as mathematics to measuring cylinder bores or crankshaft journal wear using Mercer gauges and micrometers. Nevertheless, unless a young man has a mechanical comprehension of a certain level and an arithmetic ability of a reasonable standard, he can never hope to become a skilled fitter who needs a high degree of knowledge and skill involving mathematics, mechanisms, electrical theory and manual dexterity as a basis for the maintenance of complicated and fast modern cars and commercial vehicles. It can therefore be concluded that before any boy is signed on for an apprenticeship he must be tested at a local college or by a training officer—unless of course he does possess proof of his academic ability by having 'O' levels or suitable C.S.E. passes. Having assessed the academic side of the young man's ability, other aspects which will affect his apprenticeship must also be considered.

The R.T.I.T.B. in their booklet *Recommendations for Training Apprentices* state the following requirements for apprentice selection. How these attributes can be determined are given alongside the requirement.

1. *A mechanical aptitude.* This can be ascertained by two methods. (a) a timed simple exercise in stripping down and reassembling a mechanical fuel pump, distributor or similar component in correct order. (b) a mechanical comprehension test which lasts 30 minutes or so and is completed by a technical college. This method is more scientific and gives a clear assessment.

With the first method, a practice adopted is to give the job to an experienced mechanic who, for example, completes dismantling and assembling in 15 minutes. Allowing twice this time, a candidate should complete the task in 30 minutes and the state of the finished job can give some idea of the mechanical aptitude of the boy.

The second method is used nationally and internationally. A candidate reaching a given level can be placed on a course to suit his ability.

2. *An enquiring mind.* The application form will reveal the nature of the boy's hobbies and recreation. Curiosity will be revealed if for example a boy goes kart-racing, motor cycling, caving—finding out things or showing a lively mind in the form of a hobby.

3. *Desire to become a skilled mechanic.* Whilst a boy might have ability he must be told of the dirt and hard work required to become a highly-skilled mechanic. Today's dream of white overalls and racing cars is a far cry from the reality of the underside of heavy commercial vehicles covered in dirt, oil and grease!

4. *Course of study.* This must be stressed. It is essential for a boy to attend technical college to have theoretical training in order that he can understand thoroughly his practical work. Normally attendance at a college forms part of the condition of employment of apprentices.

5. *Physical ability.* A boys health must be good to withstand some of the rigours of motor vehicle workshops. He should be fit, reasonably strong and not suffer from colour blindness if he wished to become an electrician which would mean coloured wires could not be identified correctly.

6. *Stable mentality and disposition.* This involves an assessment of a boy's personality—a complex subject. One of the best assessments of a boy's ability to mix and work with other people is his last report from school. The headmaster should be able to give a valuable assessment of a boy's character, especially if the boy has attended his last school for many years. In any event, a headmaster will generally be pleased to state how a boy has behaved During the interview, it will become fairly obvious if a boy is egotistical or modest. Certain aspects of a boy's mentality and disposition are difficult to assess completely without stringent personality tests at a college or by a training officer. However, as workshop staff work as a team, a boy should be alert, responsive to questioning and a hard worker. Hot tempered, aggressive boys can cause a good deal of upset in a workshop and these should not be encouraged to join an existing harmonious team of workers. Punctuality is very important and whether a boy can get to work on time should be ascertained from the school report or during the interview.

Now, having completed selection tests and an application form, the next step is an interview. With all details before him, the service manager can now determine a boy's general attitude, which the application form cannot reveal. For example, in reply to further questions or in outlining the work the young man will be involved with, the service manager can determine whether the boy is aggressive, cheeky, insolent, cheerful, asks reasonable questions in return, quiet and so on, bearing in mind the boy must be part of a team and therefore must be able to mix and work with other people without causing unnecessary upset.

It is the responsibility of the service manager, personnel officer or training officer of the firm to complete the process of personnel selection which in the case of apprentices is based on (a) academic suitability, (b) completion of employment application form, and (c) interview: from this a boy is either accepted or rejected.

Assuming appointment is made, the boy's future career with the firm should be carefully explained to him. For example, his training will probably start with a full-time basic motor vehicle engineering course at a local technical college, followed by further periods of training at work and at the local college for theoretical education. A chart similar to that shown in Fig. 5.4 could be used to show academic advancement and at the same time, indicate where his future lies with the firm using charts similar to Fig. 5.1 and Fig. 5.2. During the interview the R.T.I.T.B. recommend that emphasis is placed on the following items:

1. *Length of training.* This is usually 3 or 4 years and this should be explained to the boy using the R.T.I.T.B. programme shown in Fig. 5.3 to show how he will progress.

2. *Wages on starting.* The wages paid are normally determined by National Joint Industrial Council agreement. Apprentices when starting do not always share in bonus schemes and this should be explained to the newcomer if necessary so that he clearly understands what his rates of pay will be.

3. *Explanation of future prospects.* Once again, the R.T.I.T.B. programme shown in Fig. 5.3 can be used to explain prospects. In addition success in the final examinations of the City and Guilds of London Institute, courses 380 Motor Vehicle Craft Studies and 381 Light or Heavy Vehicle Mechanic, Part II, 390 Motor Vehicle Technician, 381 Vehicle Partsmen's Craft Studies Part II Practice and other related subjects can lead to supervisory jobs. Success in the final examinations of the Institute of the Motor Industry, it can be explained, often is a means of climbing up the ladder within a firm. Thus, succession and prospects could be: apprentice, fully-skilled fitter, charge-hand, foreman, reception engineer, management: all depending on work done and success in examinations. Before interviewing the boy, the parents or guardian can be consulted and all details of employment explained to them. With the parents' co-operation the firm is likely to get the best out of the boy during apprenticeship and afterwards. The apprentice is then fully aware of his future working conditions and prospects.

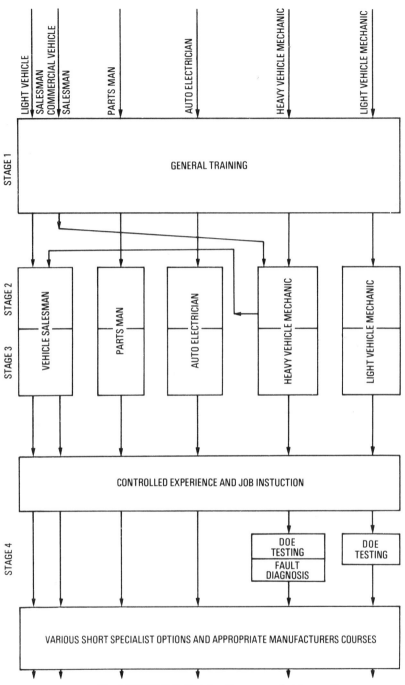

Fig. 5.3 R.T.I.T.B. Training Programme for Apprentices

AUTOMOBILE ENGINEERING PRACTICE
City and Guilds of London Institute Courses
Schemes for Motor Vehicle Mechanics, Motor Vehicle Technicians
and Parts Department Personnel

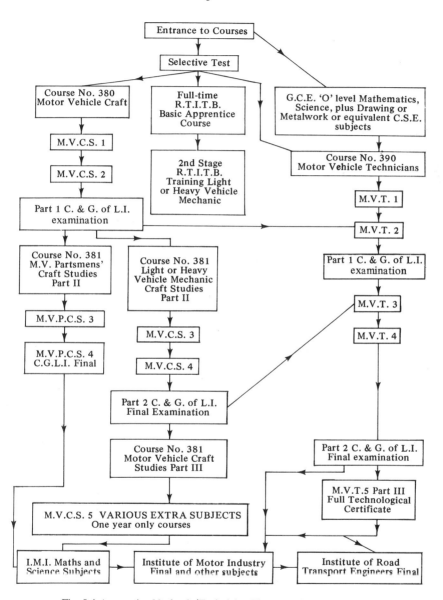

Fig. 5.4 Apprentice Mechanic/Technician Theoretical Training Chart

For notes see overleaf

Notes for Fig. 5.4

1. Entrance to the Technicians' course can also be gained by satisfactory completion of a first year General Course in Engineering.
2. Apprentices completing the basic R.T.I.T.B. and Second Stage R.T.I.T.B. will follow academic study according to their ability.
3. Parts Department Personnel will follow the route shown. Following M.V.P.C.S. 4 (Final C.G.L.I.) students will qualify for Pardic Associate Certificate and for the Advanced Pardic Certificate after I.M.I. Final.
4. The I.M.I./M.A.A. Diploma closely follows the I.M.I. final syllabus and is for mature students only.
5. Other courses include:

   379 Compression Ignition Engines Mechanics' Work Certificate
   381 Vehicle Electricians Craft Studies Part II
   381 Light Vehicle Body Repairs Craft Studies Part II
   382 Vehicle Salesmanship

Other motor vehicle courses are detailed in Appendix II.

Selection of staff for all departments

We can now consider the employment of other staff having considered the employment of apprentices and prevention of wastage.

Skilled fitters and skilled mechanics

Labour turnover is inevitable in all workshops. Staff move and wish to work nearer home, staff get promotion outside the firm and staff find better paid jobs. These are some of the reasons for staff turnover, as well as, of course, dismissal for various reasons. Thus to appoint a skilled fitter we need to know certain basic information. References can be checked by telephoning previous employers if necessary. Certainly it would be advisable to start a mechanic who has some experience of your make of vehicle. A final City and Guilds of London Institute Certificate No. 375 Motor Vehicle Mechanic or 380 and 381 and a National Craftsman Certificate (issued by the Motor Agents Association as employer representatives of the National Joint Industrial Council for the Motor Vehicle Retail and Repair Trade, but under the control of the City and Guilds of London Institute), would be very useful guides to the ability of the mechanic applying for the job.

During the interview, it is again essential to ensure the applicant will be a useful member of the firm and be able to work with other people. Questions during interview should reveal a man's general attitudes in a similar way to that of the apprentices mentioned earlier. It would also reveal why he is applying for the job, and, where applicable, the reasons for leaving his previous job or why he has been unemployed. To avoid any misunderstanding, rates of pay and conditions of service should be clearly indicated to the applicant for the job.

Semi-skilled mechanics

People of this type require some supervision on repair work. Such workers will not normally have any academic qualifications, but would have achieved some practical skill by working with skilled personnel. Appointment of such men will require some form of testimonial from a previous employer. Promotion of labourers to semi-skilled workers within a workshop can be usefully arranged, where this is warranted.

Charge-hands and foremen

It is well known that a skilled fitter who may be a first class tradesman may not necessarily make a good charge-hand or foreman. A skilled fitter can be defined as a man able to execute all repair work on a motor vehicle without supervision. Thus, a man who has had suitable training will be well able to complete this work and do it well. However, when a man is asked to take on the responsibilities of managing men and things, it requires more than the ability to execute skilled repair work, although this knowledge is an essential basic requirement of any charge-hand or foreman.

Appointment of charge-hands and foremen is almost invariably done from within a firm. An apprentice who becomes a skilled fitter and stays with the firm for a number of years will soon be noticed for his ability to execute repairs well, his punctuality, co-operative attitude, ability to work with other personnel, persistance to sort out difficult repair jobs, ability to remain cool and calm when a job demands maximum skill, patience and knowledge. All these are the attributes of a good foreman or charge-hand. When dealing with men it is vital for a foreman or charge-hand to be fair and firm at all times. During the running of any workshop, problems constantly arise: problems of a technical nature and personal problems e.g. which fitters can best do a particular job such as steering overhaul, diesel engine overhaul, gear-box or rear-axle overhaul and so on. A foreman must decide where to pass the work and the charge-hand must liaise with the foreman to ensure a smooth running of the workshop. However, let us itemize the requirements of any workshop supervisor. At this stage we can now state the essential differences between charge-hand and foreman. The foreman has overall control of the workshop including shop loading for work to be completed whilst a charge-hand will handle a small group of men, receiving work from the foreman. To ensure adequate work loads for all personnel, liaison between charge-hands and the foremen is absolutely vital. Charge-hands and foremen both manage men and offer advice to fitters and apprentices where and when required, and both need the following basic requirements:

1. A good practical background, (e.g. an apprentice-trained fitter with a minimum 3 years practical experience as a skilled fitter).
2. A good theoretical knowledge, preferably with a final City and Guilds of London Institute No. 380 with 381 or No. 390 certificate.

3. The ability to control men and work loads. To do this he must be a good organizer and have the attributes previously discussed such as pleasing personality, fairness, persistance and so on.

Before actually taking over a supervisory post it is advantageous for a potential supervisor to attend a manufacturers' course for supervisors or one organized by the R.T.I.T.B. or local technical college.

Service managers

The modern service manager needs a large amount of technical and managerial knowledge. The R.T.I.T.B. have stated the requirements of a service manager as follows:

(a)   A good practical background, i.e. an apprentice-trained mechanic or fitter.

(b)   Theoretical achievements to include a final 380/381 and 390 City and Guilds of London Institute Certificates plus a pass in the final examination of the Institute of the Motor Industry.

Equivalent certificates approved by the Department of Education and Science can be accepted in lieu of those mentioned. For example passes in the Institute of Motor Industry Part 1 or Institute of Road Transport Engineers can be accepted in place of City and Guilds of London Institute 380/381 or 390. Likewise, the M.A.A./I.M.I. Management Diploma in lieu of the final I.M.I. examinations and so on. It is, however, vital that a potential manager has a good practical and theoretical background to enable him to meet the needs and demands of a modern service station. The service manager is the hub of the station and it is upon him that success or failure will result. He must be able to motivate all staff to work together as a team. To arouse and maintain enthusiasm for the jobs in hand, to deal fairly with personnel and customers to ensure bills are delivered and paid promptly, to see that service follow-up procedures are completed are but a few of the requirements of a service manager. A detailed list of inspection duties (Vauxhall Motors Service School) and a job description form (R.T.I.T.B.) are shown in Figs 5.5 and 5.6. However, in addition to the basic theoretical knowledge required by service managers what else will go to make up an ideal service manager? Certain characteristics are essential and these can be outlined as follows:

Honesty. A service manager is in a position of trust and must therefore be honest with his employers, customers and employees. This applies to all financial aspects as well as the general approach to problems and difficulties. References from previous employers will determine this characteristic or if a service manager is appointed within a firm, his previous records should assist.

Integrity. This requirement is another vital aspect of a service manager's build-up. The way in which people at all levels are treated can make or break a firm. If a man is treated fairly even when he is wrong, he will respond much better

Date . . . .

Area	Condition			Action Taken	Responsibility	Frequency of Inspection
	Bad	Fair	Good			
S/S Approach						
Entrance						
Reception Area						
Car Wash						
Lubrication Bay						
Parts Department						
Waiting Room						
Service Mgrs. Office						
Toilets, Men						
Toilets, Ladies						
Floors						
Walls						
Windows						
Ceilings						
Work Areas						
Tool Room						
Cloak Room						
Canteen						
Lights						
Signs						
Advertising						
Personnel						
Remarks						

Fig. 5.5 Good Housekeeping Appearance and Check and Assignment Form (Vauxhall)

MANAGEMENT JOB DESCRIPTION FORM

Job Title   Service Manager

Job Location   XYZ Garage Limited,
High Street, Uxminster

Department   Service

1 MAIN PURPOSE OF THE JOB

To achieve an agreed return on the Company's investment in its workshop facilities.

To promote customer satisfaction by providing high quality service and workmanship.

To increase turnover.

2 RELATIONSHIPS

Directly responsible to –   Garage Manager

Functionally responsible to

Others with whom there are regular but
direct working relationships –

Parts Manager
Office Manager
Vehicle Sales Manager
Forecourt Supervisor

Subordinates directly supervised –

1 Workshop Controller
3 Foremen
3 Reception Engineers

Others with whom there are regular but
indirect working relationships –

Vehicle and other manufacturers
Specialist repairers
Insurance company assessors
R.T.I.T.B. Officers

3 SCOPE

The object of this section is to get into perspective the manager's main responsibilities, for example

a) Numbers Employed

Supervisors	7
Semi-skilled	10
Clerk	1
Shunter	1
Skilled staff	26
Apprentices	12
Cleaner	1

Total 58

b) Assets (e.g. vehicles, stock) if any, with indicative costs

Stock/Materials	£55,000
Equipment	£30,000
Recovery vehicles	£ 5,000

c) Any Other Responsibilities

All paperwork to be cleared weekly

Monthly check of work in progress

Preparation of new and used vehicles for retail jobs

Technical advice to Commercial and Fleet operators

Weekly check of apprentices' 'on-the-job' training programme.

4 MAJOR RESPONSIBILITIES FOR RESULTS – for example

a) Costs

To improve efficiency by monthly examination of labour and other direct costs within his control against agreed targets.

To ensure that all customer service accounts are despatched within 3 days of job completion.

To prepare a list of consumable workshop tools and materials with an estimated monthly itemised list.

b) Improved Profitability (return on capital employed)

Hours sold to be not less than 80% of productive capacity.

Gross profit percentage on labour sale to be not less than 70%.

c) Improved Job Satisfaction (to those employed)

To improve efficiency by the provision of better workshop conditions, modern equipment and tools and more opportunities for training and development.

5 LIMITS OF AUTHORITY

Financial –

All requirements to Garage Manager.

No authority to grant Credit or Discount facilities.

Personnel –

Engagement and dismissal of staff – up to but not including foremen.

Operational –

As limited by Garage Manager.

6 DESIRABLE QUALIFICATIONS, EXPERIENCE AND TRAINING

a) A sound and up-to-date knowledge of motor vehicles, including legislation and trade practices, preferably supported by documentary evidence of a National Certificate or other recognised qualifications such as Associate Member I.M.I./or M.A.A./I.M.I. Diploma.

b) An ability for administration, organisation and leadership.

Signed..................................

Date ....

Fig. 5.6 R.T.I.T.B. Service Manager Job Description

when he knows this treatment could have been expected by any member of staff who had made the same mistake.

Personality. This covers a wide range of a man's build-up. Passivity, aggression, vitality, enthusiasm, pessimist, are some of the characteristics which go to build up the personality of a man. A service manager needs to be pleasing in appearance and in speech, enthusiastic, and calm in the face of difficulties.

Ability. This has already been defined, but whilst academic attainment is vital, the other factors, honesty, integrity and personality also form a large part of a service manager's make-up. Once having been trained, a manager must be able to use his theoretical knowledge in a practical way to run a service station efficiently. The monthly Profit and Loss Account will soon determine this factor. Consequently, a manufacturers' course such as those run by Vauxhall Motors, Ford Marketing Institute and B.L.M.C. will be extremely valuable aids to train a man to meet the needs of his particular products. The R.T.I.T.B. and local technical colleges also run short courses to assist potential managers, but these do not replace the detailed and required knowledge of the final examinations of the I.M.I., M.A.A., or I.R.T.E.

Parts managers, forecourt managers, car sales managers

Having considered in some detail the requirements of a service manager, the requirements of other managers will be similar, but with ability slanted in their particular direction. For example, a parts department manager must have had a good practical parts training and attained an Advanced Pardic Certificate, a forecourt manager will require a similar background to a car sales manager who, in turn, must have passed the appropriate sections of the I.M.I. final syllabuses. Again, courses by manufacturers and the R.T.I.T.B. are very useful aids to managers specializing in a particular field.

Reception engineers (service advisers)

The responsibilities of a reception engineer also referred to in some garages as service adviser, are discussed in Chapter 3. Qualifications for such posts should include (a) good practical workshop background (b) theoretical attainment to final City and Guilds of London Institute 380/381 (minimum) whilst final 390 is to be preferred. Remembering that receptionists meet the customer and consequently represent the garage, a vital part of any reception engineer is a pleasing personality. Customers can be very difficult sometimes and frequently give obscure instructions. A service adviser must, therefore, have the ability to mix and meet all kinds of people and have a personality similar to that of a good foreman.

Office staff

Office staff will be appointed according to the needs of the garage. A qualified accountant will run all the firms accounts and also be responsible for ensuring suitable staff are appointed to meet the special skills of office work, e.g. typists, clerks, computer operators, etc.

Cleaners

For workshops and other areas cleaners need no special skills, but they do need to feel they are an essential part of the service station operations. No special forms are needed, but essential basic details must be taken such as full name and address, age, health. Rates of pay must be clearly indicated and any profit-sharing schemes explained. It is vital that cleaners do understand the importance of clean workshop floors as an aid to accident prevention and here the service manager appointing can use his personality to motivate a cleaner to work with the minimum of supervision. Similarly, the ability of a cleaner to work with people and not against them is essential and should be stressed. The actual duties of a cleaner, as with other posts, should be very clearly defined to avoid jobs not being done or repeated, and prevent misunderstandings and loss of work output.

A similar technique must be adopted for labourers in the workshop and other areas.

Interview techniques

This chapter has dealt with selection of staff for different posts and the needs of each job have been outlined. Before any interview takes place to appoint any person for a job, basic information and more detailed information where required is obtained. The object of the interview is to assess parts of a persons character and personality which an application form can not.

For positions up to foreman, service advisers, chargehands, mechanics, apprentices and cleaners, the service manager will generally appoint, but he may have the assistance of another manager so that two will sit on the employers side to interview the applicant. Obviously, questions will be pre-written on a separate sheet with blank spaces for the service manager to write in the applicant's verbal replies. Questions will be framed to bring out special knowledge or attitudes. For example, in the appointment of a foreman, a question to determine an applicant's attitude upon discovering a mistake could be as follows: 'You have found an oil filter has not been changed and the car has been allowed out of the workshop. What action would you take against the mechanic?' An immediate 'sack him' would obviously reveal a lack of ability or interest to obtain details of why the filter change was missed. If it had been done deliberately, obviously a mechanic would have to have a severe warning at least because of the serious position in which he had placed the company. The reply would reveal many of the personality traits referred to earlier in the chapter. Therefore, when interviewing, questions must be written with an object in mind but the applicant should be given time to ask for any further details about the post so that he knows fully what his duties will be.

Committee interviews. Usually these are reserved for management posts. At least two or three senior members of a firm will interview candidates in turn, usually alphabetically so that discrimination is avoided. Depending on the importance of the post, for example, a senior service manager, could expect an interview to last at least 30 minutes. Candidates would be shown around the workshops and a general assessment of bearing, speech, dress, attitudes etc., made during this period of time. Finally, the successful candidate will be brought back to the interview room and appointed. There are many reasons for this interview technique, but basically it is to obtain the right man for the job. So many things are revealed: for example the man who must loudly proclaim what he has done is not likely to be any better than the quiet man who has achieved exactly the same but with increased efficiency and without upsetting the entire staff. Appointment of senior posts, it may be mentioned here, can be from within a firm or from outside. From within a worthy man should be considered, but not from length of service only. A man from outside can inject new ideas, prevent stagnation and has the advantage of not being known on a personal level to the people he is to manage.

Training programmes: road transport industry training board

Training programmes and the R.T.I.T.B. must be mentioned together, for it is the Board who have instituted, recommended and generally brought about excellent training programmes for all members of the staff of all service stations. Unless suitable training programmes are instituted and trained competent staff obtained, service stations must surely go out of existence. The general public expect a good service but have, unfortunately, received very poor service from many. Not all service stations should be labelled as such because some have been very progressive indeed having training programmes for all staff before the R.T.I.T.B. came into existence in 1966/7. No progressive person can dispute that good training must result in better personnel and, in turn, more efficiency with resulting increased profitability for the service station. So it now is a fact that apprentices undergo training which is properly planned, laid out in correct and detailed form, and the employer and apprentice has an Apprentice Log Book issued and inspected by Training Officers of the R.T.I.T.B. Details of apprentice training recommended by the R.T.I.T.B. can be found in the Boards booklet *Training Recommendations for Motor Vehicle Mechanics.* Similarly, training recommendations and requirements for all other staff can be found in the R.T.I.T.B. booklets.

To obtain grants from the R.T.I.T.B. to which all employers pay a levy according to the size of the wage bill, training programmes must be strictly adhered to, that is a certain part of training must be completed within a certain period of time. Technical colleges are operating workshops for basic training facilities within their own workshops to meet the R.T.I.T.B. requirements.

Training Officers from the Board are always willing to offer expert advice about any aspect of training.

Manufacturers of cars and commercial vehicles have and still are providing first class training programmes for special aspects of motor vehicle trades. For example, engine overhaul, automatic transmission, parts department procedures, service managers' courses, body repair course, brake system overhaul, car sales course, in fact almost every aspect of car repair and subsequent sales is covered by the car manufacturers in this country. Application to attend such courses must be made to the manufacturer concerned. As all such courses are invariably recommended and approved by the R.T.I.T.B. full grants are paid to employers sending employees on such courses. As vehicle manufacturing processes change resulting in better vehicles each year, employees must from time to time attend refresher courses in order to bring themselves up to date and retain their efficiency as employees of a firm. The service manager or training officer of a firm must arrange attendance on such courses by employees who need such training.

Wage structures

This important topic is not an easy one to put out in an order to suit each geographical area of Britain. The law of supply and demand varies wages throughout the country, likewise the cost of living which, for example, is more expensive in central London than say in Liverpool or Manchester.

However, a basic wage scale for apprentices and mechanics is agreed between the Motor Agents Association on the employers side and Trade Unions on the employees side. These bodies, along with other representatives, sit on the National Joint Industrial Council for the Motor Vehicle Retail and Repair Trade. Thus, the M.A.A. and the unions decide the minimum basic rates of pay, number of hours worked per week, holidays, apprentice agreements and other factors affecting employees of service stations. Minimum rates of pay are the agreed rates because as stated previously, a minimum rate of pay say of 50p per hour for a mechanic in the north of England would not be acceptable in central London because of the cost of living. Unless higher rates are paid, mechanics will move to better paid jobs in order to have a reasonable standard of living.

To obtain a structure of wages will depend upon the minimum rates agreed by the N.J.I.C.R.R.T. for apprentices and full-skilled mechanics whilst semi-skilled and unskilled workers also have agreed rates of pay. For the moment we will not consider incentive schemes.

Now if we state for example that a fully-skilled mechanic has a basic rate of 50p per hour for a 42 hour week (5 day week), then the mechanic will receive £21 basic pay. An unskilled worker will receive say, £15 and a semi-skilled worker £18. Upon basic wages we must now add appropriate allowances for responsibility. A wage structure for a garage could be similar to that shown overleaf.

Let £x = A skilled mechanic's weekly rate

16 year old apprentice : Commences at $\frac{1}{3}$£x rising by increments to skilled
 mechanic rate.

	Minimum rates	Possible rates
Skilled mechanic	£x	£1.25x
Charge-hand	£1.1x	£1.4x
Foreman	£1.25x	£1.6x
Reception engineer	£1.25x	£1.6x
Service manager	£1.75x	£2.5x

In some service stations, foremen, reception engineers and service managers
are regarded as staff positions and will, therefore, have an annual rate quoted,
for example, service manager (£2.5x) 52 per year. Payment during sickness is
usually automatic for such posts. Rates of pay must vary according to basic
rates for mechanics and the extent of responsibility for a particular post. A
service manager in charge of 15 staff will obviously not be paid the same rate
for a man controlling 150 staff. As service work becomes more streamlined,
e.g. flow-line servicing, use of sophisticated testing machines and so on, it is
quite possible for mechanics to have a flat rate much higher than at present,
with service managers commanding a salary in excess of (£4x) 52 a year for top
posts.

Incentive schemes

The basic rates of pay require some means of reward to improve productivity. Most workshops now use the basic hourly rates for jobs, arranged by
manufacturers by time and motion study methods, as a means of payment of
incentive money. For example, a service job requiring 3 hours work, completed
in 2 hours by a mechanic means 1 hour saved. Thus, a mechanic gets 3 hours
pay for 2 hours work and immediately starts on another job. The customer of
course pays for 3 hours work and the workshop must profit from time saved.
In fact, many workshops now expect mechanics to be earning a minimum of
10 hours bonus per week as this increases profit from the workshop.

Overtime rates are agreed as per basic rates and incentive bonus operates the
same.

Tool-kits can be supplied to mechanics at trade prices or less as an incentive
for completing so many bonus hours or for any other reason which a firm may
decide upon such as so many weeks without being late or absent. Such schemes
are called *financial* incentive schemes. Free holidays for the most work output
have also been financial incentive schemes tried successfully.

Profit sharing schemes. These have now become a very popular means of
financial incentive awards. Part of the total profit for a workshop is proportioned out to all employees from cleaners, labourers, mechanics and so on
in relation to their rate of pay. Everyone is made to feel part of a team know-
ing that the quicker a job is completed and completed well the more money
is going to be in their pay packet. Wastage of split-pins, nuts and bolts, oils

etc., is kept to a minimum because employees are made aware that such items will be costed against the workshop operation and result in less profit and less money in the pay packet.

Non-financial incentive schemes. Such schemes are those in which money is not directly involved. Under this heading comes free overalls laundered twice a week, free tea breaks, social outings, use of sports and social club amenities, free transport to and from work to mention a few.

Financial and non-financial schemes must assist in keeping staff, providing they are fairly operated, which is the direct responsibility of management. Mismanagement of such schemes must result in disgruntled staff with poor work output and large staff turnover which reduces profits because of the extra advertising costs and training costs involved.

Formulating an incentive scheme for mechanics and other personnel

We have seen that as an aid to productivity a scheme has to be devised to encourage personnel to work hard and efficiently. To enable a fair system to operate so that all personnel are treated the same some garages have a card which details many characteristics of a man's ability to get an all round picture of a man's productivity. A number of points are given for each attribute, and, depending upon the number of points a man obtains, a rate of pay is subsequently awarded. Let us itemize some of the attributes which go to make up a good worker and allocate a number of points for each of these characteristics:

(a)	Ability in his trade	120
(b)	Productivity and effiency	40
(c)	Reliability	40
(d)	Cleanliness	40
(e)	Timekeeping	20
(f)	Knowledge of vehicles	40
(g)	Extra trades ability	40
(h)	Driving ability	20
(i)	Academic qualifications	40
	Maximum total possible points	400

Now these items can be put on a card with a space underneath to award the actual points for a particular asset as shown in Fig. 5.7. The service manager will record the actual marks scored (probably on a 3 or 6 monthly basis) so that a rate of pay can be established.

When scoring the card a mechanic could score points on the following lines:

(a)   *Ability in trade*

      (1) Able to complete all repairs without supervision and conversant with modern equipment for diagnosing and rectifying faults.

                                    Score = maximum points i.e. 120

    (2) Requires some supervision. Deduct 20 points.   Score = 100

    (3) Has reasonable skill but requires more training and
        experience. Deduct 30 points.   Score = 90

    (4) Semi-skilled and needs supervision. Deduct 40 points. Score = 80

(b) *Productivity and efficiency*

    (1) Productivity record over the past 3 months is in excess
        of 100%. Does not waste time and is always looking for
        extra work. Looks for better methods for completing
        repairs.   Score = maximum points i.e. 40

    (2) Has 90% plus productivity record over the past 3 months
        and looks for extra work. Deduct 6 points.   Score = 34

    (3) Below 90% productivity record over the past 3 months
        and continually requires supervision to get work done.
        Deduct 14 points.   Score = 26

(c) *Reliability*

    (1) Faulty work not known. Will report any extra work
        needed on a vehicle on his own initiative.
                Score = maximum points i.e. 40

    (2) Work returned occasionally for correction.
        Deduct 6 points.   Score = 34

    (3) Work returned for correction several times and does not
        report extra work needed on a vehicle unless asked.
        Deduct 20 points.   Score = 20

(d) *Cleanliness*

    (1) Always clean and tidy in appearance. Keeps work areas
        clean and tidy. Uses seat, wing and steering wheel covers.
                Score = maximum points i.e. 40

    (2) Always clean in personal appearance but tends to leave
        tools and parts in untidy state. Uses covers to protect
        vehicles. Deduct 10 points.   Score = 30

    (3) Requires constant reminding about cleanliness and
        importance of safety with oil not cleaned from floor,
        etc. Parts left about and tools not cleaned properly.
        Deduct 25 points.   Score = 15

(e) *Timekeeping*

    (1) Always on time and ready to start work.
             Score = maximum points i.e. 20

    (2) Arrives on time but starts work after time.
        Deduct 10 points.   Score = 15

    (3) Generally on time but has a number of late starts during
        a month.
        Deduct 20 points.   Score = 10

(f) *Knowledge of vehicles*
    (1) Good up-to-date knowledge of vehicles which he is working
        on e.g. Vauxhall, B.M.C., Ford, etc. Has obtained good
        passes in Factory Courses which he has attended say 6 in
        last 3 years (2 each year)

                                Score = maximum points i.e.   40
    (2) A fairly good knowledge of vehicles with passes in Factory
        Courses attended.
        Deduct 10 points.   Score = 30
    (3) Requires pressing to read up-to-date literature on vehicle
        repairs and needs improving generally.
        Deduct 20 points.   Score = 20

(g) *Extra trades ability*
    (1) Can do extra work such as good quality repair welding,
        fit body trims, etc.

                                Score = maximum points i.e.   40
    (2) Can do extra work under supervision.
        Deduct 15 points.   Score = 25

(h) *Driving ability*
    (1) Good driver—no accidents over past 12 months. Ability
        to use driving knowledge in diagnosing faults.

                                Score = maximum points i.e.   20
    (2) As above except 6 months accident free record.
        Deduct 6 points.   Score = 14
    (3) Has driving licence but cannot use his ability in road test
        diagnostic work owing to lack of experience.
        Deduct 10 points.   Score = 10

(i) *Academic qualifications*
    (1) Holds C.G.L.I. 390 Final or Full Technological Certificate.
                                Score = maximum points i.e.   40
    (2) Holds C.G.L.I. 380/381 Final and National Craftsman
        Certificate.
        Deduct 12 points.   Score = 28
    (3) Holds C.G.L.I. 380/381 Final.
        Deduct 10 points.   Score = 20
    (4) Holds Factory Certificates—4 points for each to maximum
        of 20 points.

By breaking down an incentive scheme in this way a fair system of incentive
can be awarded to mechanics and disputes avoided. Depending upon the number of points obtained a mechanic's rate of pay will be determined. For example
a rate of pay on the merit points gained could be as follows:

Pay scales for mechanics

Points	380–400	360–379	340–359	320–339	300–319	
Pay per hour	£1	£0.97	£0.95	£0.93	£0.90	
Points	290–299	280–289	270–279	260–269	250–259	Below 250
Pay per hour	£0.89	£0.87	£0.86	£0.85	£0.84	£0.80

The mechanic will be presented with a card similar to that shown in Fig. 5.6 and his rate of pay indicated.

Whilst this system does involve a lot of initial work, once it has been established a fair system of incentive pay will operate especially where a large number of mechanics are employed. The special needs of each garage could be included in such a scheme and items not considered essential deleted. It will be the responsibility of the service manager to decide finally what will make up his incentive scheme in order to improve and maintain efficiency in his workshops and other departments.

Whatever scheme is devised the basic essentials of a good incentive wage plan are:

1. A guaranteed minimum wage must be ensured.
2. The plan must be fair and just to employer and employee.
3. Employees and employer must support the plan.
4. All standards set must be based on a time study or, alternatively, on realistic attributes of personnel.
5. The plan must be as simple as possible so that an employee can determine his potential earnings.
6. The incentive must be correct in detail; if the standard set is high, the reward must be generous.
7. No restriction on earnings should be imposed.
8. The plan must assist good work and, if possible, aid team work.
9. Costing of the plan should be as simple as possible.
10. Any standards set must be guaranteed against change unless methods alter.

In implementing any plan a student should remember that it is easy to lose money and be popular. The incentive scheme used must result in greater productivity in the workshop which, in turn, means higher wage packets and higher profits for the service station.

Questions

1. Most manufacturers issue standard times for service work. Some issue standard charges. How would you ensure that these times and charges are kept and what action would you take when you find that the time has been grossly exceeded. (I.M.I.)

Name of Mechanic:

For Month:

Year:

Ability with trade	Productivity and efficiency	Reliability	Cleanliness
Max. 120	Max. 40	Max. 40	Max. 40
Actual	Actual	Actual	Actual
Timekeeping	Knowledge of vehicles	Extra trades ability	Driving ability
Max. 20	Max. 40	Max. 40	Max. 20
Actual	Actual	Actual	Actual
Academic qualifications			
Max. 40			
Actual			

Total max. = 400

Actual   =

Hourly rate of pay =

Signed . . . .

SERVICE MANAGER

Date . . . .

Fig. 5.7 Incentive Scheme Card

2. In some establishments a lot of time is spent in obtaining material from the parts department. How would you operate your workshop to cut this time down to a reasonable minimum, bearing in mind that there must be a proper record of all parts issued? (I.M.I.)

3. It is now a well established principle to pay an incentive bonus to all repair-shop personnel. As a service manager, what type of scheme would you employ. (I.M.I.)

4. As it is most important to recruit the right personnel for staff positions such as reception engineers or shop foremen, state what characteristics you would look for and what questions you would ask when interviewing an applicant for either of the two posts mentioned. (I.M.I.)

5. Many firms have clearly printed forms showing the conditions of service. As a service manager say what you consider such conditions should be. (I.M.I.)

6. Discuss the following from the point of view of retaining skilled labour.
   (a) Direct payment—higher rates of pay.
   (b) Financial incentives, i.e. bonus or similar schemes.
   (c) Non-financial incentives. (I.M.I.)

7. Describe any 'Bonus Scheme', 'Merit Pay' or any other 'production incentive' which you know as being fair to all concerned, i.e. customer, the employer and the employee. (I.M.I.)

8. Large organizations frequently appoint a personnel officer, one of whose duties is to help employees with their problems. In smaller organizations this usually falls on the manager's shoulders. Do you consider it is a good policy to render welfare assistance to employees and state your reasons whether yes or no. (I.M.I.)

9. Selection of personnel for a particular job is extremely important. State the requirements you would expect when appointing—
   (a) An apprentice mechanic
   (b) A skilled fitter
   (c) A foreman
   (d) A service manager. (I.M.I.)

10. Skilled mechanics are still in short supply in the retail motor trade. Semi-skilled mechanics are a little easier to obtain. Suggest a practical method through which semi-skilled men can gain the necessary experience and knowledge to qualify for higher grading while remaining in employment. (I.M.I.)

CHAPTER 6

FORECOURT WORK

Forecourt management

The forecourt area of any service station is one which must attract the attention of potential customers. It is essential to arrange that the forecourt is cleaned every day, petrol pumps and oil pumps are wiped clean, windows are cleaned, advertisements are kept clean and up-to-date, accessories are well displayed, customers have good access to the forecourt, toilet signs are displayed clearly and staff are trained for their jobs. Forecourts usually are concerned with petrol, oil and accessory sales and it is these with which we shall concern ourselves. As the staff to operate a forecourt are of prime importance, we can consider this aspect first.

Forecourt manager

As explained in Chapter 5 any manager needs to have a good background for his particular area of operation. The sale of parts, accessories, petrol and oil demands a thorough knowledge of parts mechandising and management techniques. Thus, a forecourt manager, ideally would possess the M.A.A./I.M.I. diploma. In addition he would also require the personal qualities of honesty, integrity, ability and have a pleasing personality. His personality should be such as to motivate his staff to keep the forecourt and accesssory area in first class condition. It is the manager who will make out his profit and loss account and he will depend a great deal on his staff to ensure a profit is made. Staff must, therefore, be made aware that spillage of oil, breakage of accessories and so on all mean loss. Profit sharing schemes help to achieve the right attitude and can be very usefully employed.

Forecourt staff

Manning the petrol pumps and accessory shops on a service station forecourt is an important job. This job has traditionally been regarded as unskilled and, therefore, anyone is allowed to sell petrol and parts. The result of this negative thinking has been a very high staff changeover rate: it is difficult to retain people for over 3 months.

According to a published survey, forecourt staff were rated—'50% lazy, 40% dishonest, 10% useless': no praise at all for anyone who had been employed! Most forecourt staff had a combined tendency of laziness *and* dishonesty: what a sad picture! Who should be blamed for this state of affairs? Well, who appointed them and arranged the conditions of service?—managers of course! When conditions of service are poor what kind of staff is the job likely to attract? In any event, conditions and payment should be made attractive so that reasonable staff will be obtained and profits will increase. The customer has a right to good service for his money and he will certainly go where his custom is appreciated. *If* the right staff are recruited a forecourt can prove to be a highly profitably area, but the right staff must first be obtained. What are the requirements of a member of the forecourt staff? Would he be useful if he attended the Vehicle Partsmen's Craft Studies Part II City and Guilds of London Institute Course No. 381 at technical college? The size of the station and the parts department would enable a man to decide if attendance for such a course would be justified. Mostly, forecourt staff don't need such detailed knowledge as is required by the parts department staff, but forecourt staff need to know:

1. How to operate petrol pumps and oil pumps.
2. How to unlock various types of bonnets.
3. The positions of dipsticks in various engines, correct oil levels, grades of oil.
4. Correct water levels for radiators and batteries, correct dilutions of anti-freeze and water mixtures for anti-corrosion purposes and prevention of frost damage.
5. The types of radial and cross-ply tyres available, the air pressures for different cars, and how to use air pressure equipment safely.
6. The range of accessories available in the forecourt shop.
7. How to complete money addition quickly and accurately.
8. How to use fire extinguishers for fire control: a working knowledge of first aid would also be a valuable asset.

This basic list could be added to or reduced to suit individual cases. In any event the duties of the staff can be listed and, whilst they are not very demanding in skill, it is essential for all staff to be able to satisfactorily deal with the points covered. Thus, suitable training must be given and a course of instruction is available at the M.O.T.E.C. establishment in Shropshire, which is operated by the R.T.I.T.B. Some technical colleges also provide similar courses.

In addition to the knowledge required:

1. Staff must be punctual and understand shift work rotas for days off.
2. They must be smart and clean in appearance. This is in part accomplished by the manager supplying fresh overalls every 2 days or so.
3. Staff must be tidy and keep the forecourt tidy. The forecourt area must be kept clean and free from obstructions at all times to avoid accidents and give a good impression to customers.

4. Customers must be served in correct rotation as quickly and courteously as possible.

5. Staff must remain pleasant at all times and preserve good customer relationships by a friendly approach. A smile and a courteous 'good morning' or 'good afternoon' can help a great deal.

Given a knowledgeable and friendly approach to customers, a good forecourt salesman can easily assist profitability. A new accessory can be mentioned in passing and always a 'thank you' for any sale, whether it is petrol, oil or accessory should be automatic.

Cleaners

Where cleaners are employed, they should have clear instructions about their duties. The concrete floor of the forecourt for example will need to be washed down every morning. Pumps should be wiped down and polished. Toilets should be kept scrupulously clean and stocked. Windows should be polished and cleaned each day. Cleaners should be encouraged so that they are aware of the importance of their part in the profitability of the station. A dirty and untidy forecourt can turn customers away and cleaners should be reminded of the fact.

Cashiers

Some petrol forecourts—especially the self service type—employ a cashier who handles money only. As the automated pumps record the amount delivered on the console in the office, the cashier takes the money from the customer and hands him a receipt if required. The cashier usually gives trading stamps, gifts and so on according to the amount of petrol purchased so she must be fully aware of these arrangements. The ability to handle money well is essential. An efficient manager will be able to tabulate at any given moment all petrol sales and cross-check money in the till. Some stations make the cashier responsible for all shortages and the cashier has this amount deducted from his or her wages.

Control and costing of petrol sales

As with all other departments a Profit and Loss account must be made to ensure this part of the station is making adequate profits. There are a number of factors to be considered when making up the account. The cost of running this department would be made up as follows:

(1)   rates and rent for building and land,
(2)   electricity used for pumps and lighting,
(3)   wages for all staff,
(4)   purchase of petrol, oil accesories,
(5)   advertising and printing costs,
(6)   cost of trading stamps and gifts (if any),
(7)   maintenance of pumps and buildings,
(8)   evaporation losses of petrol (maximum = 2%).

On the credit side would be the sale of petrol, oil and accessories. Petrol profits are not high and great care and control must be exercised over the staff. For example, when the delivery of petrol takes place, the tanker should stand for 15 minutes before a dip reading is taken so that the fuel is not turbulent and giving a high reading resulting in a loss during delivery. The station tanks should be checked before and after delivery, the latter only after the petrol has settled in the tanks. Some tankers now have a metered system which can be checked. Besides the practice of checking actual delivery, the station tanks must be able to take the proposed load of petrol and the tanker driver will demand a signature to this effect—e.g. 'No. 1 tank 500 gallons'—hence the need to check the station tanks before delivery.

Actual delivery of fuel through the pumps can be checked daily by the meters. Each pump checked along with cash taken means a good control of all sales.

Where an account is at the petrol station, sales are recorded on an account form and total sales added up at the end of the month. A very useful account sheet available from Kalamazoo Ltd., and is shown in Fig. 6.1. Keeping these forms in alphabetical order in the office provides an accurate check of petrol, oil and accessories sales, along with the customer's signature. At the end of the month the second or duplicate copy is sent to the customer as a bill and payment is then made.

Self-service petrol stations

A fairly recent innovation has been customers serving themselves with petrol. This has certain advantages to the customer and the garage. For the garage it offers:
1. Reduction in staff
2. Increased custom, with increase in petrol, oil and accessory sales.
For the customer self-service offers:
1. Cheaper petrol in the form of trading stamps and gifts or some form of discount
2. Speedy service.

Self-service disadvantages for the station are nil unless, of course, initial training of customers to use the pumps to obtain correct octane and amount of fuel could be considered. For the customer, the smell of petrol on his hands, especially if he is going out and is not dressed for such work, having to get out of the car, complexity of instructions on pump operation, absence of friendly personal attention, are the price of cheaper fuel, increased speed. However, the general public have taken well to such stations and the layout of some of these is now described.

Layout of self-service petrol stations

This is best considered from the ergonomic point of view, a) the customer must fill his own tank, b) more than one customer may want to do so at once.

Petrol pumps can still be found standing very close together on conventional stations which means that access can be gained to one pump only, and, at the same time, the adjacent pump is rendered useless as another car cannot get

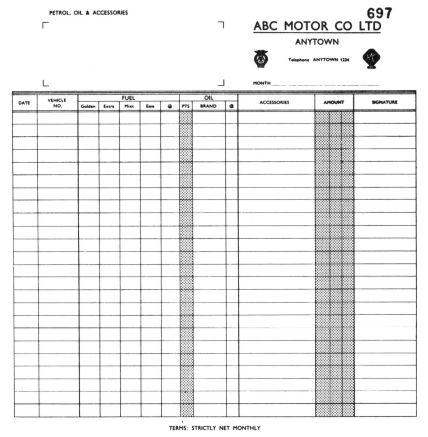

Fig. 6.1 Customer's Petrol Account

near to it. This is illustrated in Fig. 6.2. Self-service stations have well set-out forecourts with access for a car on either side of a pump. A typical layout is shown in Fig. 6.3. Adequate room is allowed in each lane for cars to move along and obtain a flow of cars by having one direction only and not the confused situation of cars entering from both sides, creating blockages and a danger of accidents. Thus, with the pump islands spaced as shown along with one way traffic, a flow-line of petrol fill-up is obtained. With high density of traffic this type of station can be very profitable and, indeed, essential in some cases for the station to exist with the fierce competition in this field.

Whilst operating on the same principle, self-service stations now exist where the pump islands have been removed with the intention of reducing the possibility of accidents. It has been found that vehicle flow has increased by having overhead pump nozzles which are lowered electrically and can be lowered manually in the event of a power failure. The ground surrounding the nozzle area is clearly marked in coloured paint to indicate octane and grades of petrol. This type of arrangement has been very effective in other countries, Japan for example, has over 2 000 such installations.

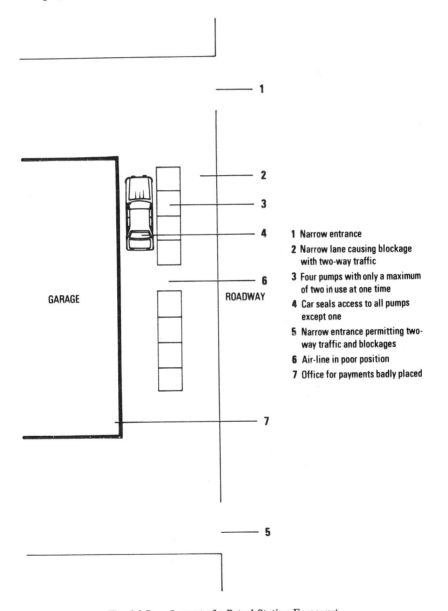

1 Narrow entrance

2 Narrow lane causing blockage with two-way traffic

3 Four pumps with only a maximum of two in use at one time

4 Car seals access to all pumps except one

5 Narrow entrance permitting two-way traffic and blockages

6 Air-line in poor position

7 Office for payments badly placed

Fig. 6.2 Poor Layout of a Petrol Station Forecourt

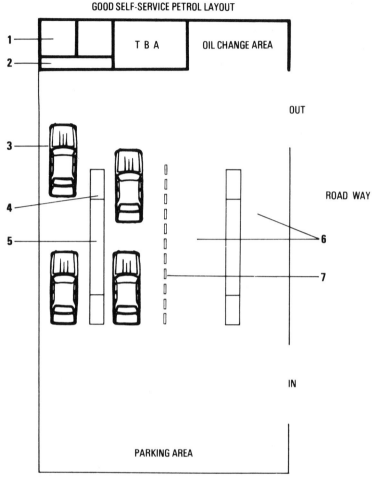

GOOD SELF-SERVICE PETROL LAYOUT

1 Office with master switch
2 Console to record gallonage and price
3 Cars with access to a single or double pump from either side
4 Blender pump to deliver up to 50 litres (11 gallons) per minute
5 Island holding central air line - accessible to all cars
6 Clear lanes at least 2 metres (6·56 feet) wide
7 Painted white line to indicate lane

One way traffic arrangement to speed flow and prevent blockages Petrol tanks with capacity up to 55000 litres (2000 gallons) are encased in concrete below ground A canopy will normally cover the filling up area Water for radiators and batteries will be available on the pump islands T B A shop provides useful addition to profit of station Fire fighting apparatus should be placed at points recommended by local fire station officer

Fig. 6.3 Layout of a Self-Service Petrol Station Forecourt

Unattended self-service stations have been installed throughout Britain. At the present time about 200 unattended stations exist. To obtain petrol, a £1 note is placed in the machine, the customer then goes to the nearest petrol pump and petrol to the value of £1 is delivered. The advantage of such arrangements are as follows:

1. no staff required,
2. service can operate 24 hours a day,
3. maximum profit on sales when trading stamps and gifts are not given—especially with night service.

At the time of writing, the largest self-service station in the world exists on the North Circular Road at Edmonton in London. This has 8 self-service pumps, can deal with 500 cars per hour dispensing 9 000 litres (2 000 gallons) of petrol per hour, requires a staff of two only to run the station, has computerized blending pumps which can increase octane value by steps of 1.25 with corresponding increase of price, supplies octane sheets with each car listed so that the customer knows what to put in his tank and the station itself covers an area of approximately 1 250 square metres (1 500 square yards). Needless to say, such a layout must have traffic density similar to that found on the North Circular Road. For such stations the underground tanks must also be of good size such as 25 000 litres (5 500 gallons) capacity or more.

One further idea with self-service stations is the provision of fast and slow lanes, slow lanes providing air lines for checking tyre pressures, distilled water for batteries, adequate time for oil checks and so on whilst still providing a speedy service depending on the customer himself. Fast lanes provide for petrol sales only. Combined self-service and 'service' lanes have been provided to meet the needs of all customers: those wishing to fill up themselves and perhaps obtain trading stamps or discount and those who prefer to pay a little more for personal attention. The choice of station will depend upon the needs of each area, but as in the author's opinion, self-service is here to stay and approximately half the petrol sold will be dispensed by this method in the mid 1970's, self-service must receive very serious consideration from those considering the construction of new service stations.

The law and the forecourt

It is not intended to detail the law affecting the forecourt, but as the running of a forecourt can be seriously affect by old and recent legislation, a brief survey of important aspects of the law must be considered.

Petroleum (Regulations Acts 1928 and 1936)

All managers must have a detailed knowledge of these regulations with up-to-date amendments, which can be obtained from H.M.S.O. Some special points from these regulations are as follows:

1. No petrol is to be served in containers other than steel cans painted red

and marked clearly with the word 'Petrol'.

2. A master switch inaccessible to the public should be provided in a suitable position so that supplies can be cut-off instantly.

3. No stop must be fitted on the nozzle which would enable the valve to be kept fully open without manual control.

4. Power connections to the pumps should be to the satisfaction of the local authorities and all metal enclosures to the pumps should be efficiently earthed.

5. Each pump should have a fuse or circuit breaker for its electrical circuit and such fuses or circuit breakers should be outside the pump-equipment housing.

6. The maximum delivery of petrol where the public have access should at one delivery not exceed 50 litres (11 gallons). Up to 136.5 litres (30 gallons) for one delivery is allowed on premises where the public have no access.

7. In normal installations, maximum pump delivery pressure should not exceed 0.206 N/mm^2 (30 lbf/in^2) and, where sight glasses are provided, these should be capable of withstanding a hydrostatic pressure of 0.512 N/mm^2 (75 lbf/in^2).

8. Enclosure of pump motors should be flameproof, likewise all switches and relays.

9. Lighting fittings mounted on the outside of pumps should be sealed to prevent the ingress of petrol vapour.

10. All cables should be enclosed in heavy gauge galvanized solid drawn steel conduit and all joints treated to prevent ingress of water.

11. A 'no smoking' sign, to conform with the petroleum regulation requirements for size and colour, should be prominently displayed.

12. Staff should not wear steel-tipped shoes or boots.

13. Adequate fire-fighting apparatus must be available on site and be approved by the local fire station officer. Local licensing authorities have their own local requirements and they should be consulted for advice and for details of any local restrictions. For example, it is illegal in some areas for tankers to discharge their load whilst parked under the canopy of the station. As stated previously, tanker drivers must also get a certificate signed before they discharge their load, stating that the tank can take the load they are about to deliver. All managers should have a copy of the petroleum regulations and be conversant with local requirements of the licensing authority.

Weights and Measures Act (1963)

Each pump is inspected periodically by local officers from the weights and measures department of the local council. Pumps are checked for delivery and duly sealed by the officers. Interference with such seals will result in prosecution. No shortage on the measured imperial gallon is allowed and only one fluid ounce above the imperial gallon is acceptable: for pumps dispensing in litres the allowance is ± 10 ml per litre or 0.05% of the volume delivered. Petrol pump and oil pump delivery is governed by the Measuring Instruments (Liquid Fuel and Oil) Regulations 1929. The construction of all tanks, piping, valves, pumps etc. must comply to Board of Trade requirements.

Trade Descriptions Act (1969)

This Act deals with the honesty of a trader. Any advertisement or offer of sale or service must be strictly correct. If not, prosecution could result. For example, if a certain oil is offered at 20p per 5 litres (9 pints) below retail price, then it must be exactly 20p below the price. Very careful scrutiny of all advertising must be made to ensure it is a true and honest statement.

Town and Country Planning Act (Control of Advertisements amendment 1970)

Hitherto, advertisements on forecourts has been virtually unrestricted. In many cases the result has been a tendency towards garish and distasteful forecourt frontages. The control of advertisements has now been made a legal requirement and this Act generally deals basically with taste. Restriction on size and quantity of advertising is now controlled by local council officers who will advise on the advertising permissible for any forecourt area.

To conclude this chapter it is essential to remember that many petrol stations are owned by major oil and petrol companies. A great deal of useful advice can be obtained from the oil companies when considering all aspects of forecourt design and management.

Having read the theory of operation of a forecourt, students would assist themselves a great deal by visiting a successful station by arrangement with the proprietors to find out how theory is put into practice. Before the visit a student could make out a questionnaire similar to the following:

1. Detail the checks made by the weights and measures departments when they visit this station.
2. Itemize the costs of running a petrol station.
3. The Petroleum Regulations govern the sale of petrol. List the regulations which this station consider imperative.
4. What gallonage will each pump give at one operation and how many octanes are available?
5. Detail the normal running of a petrol station on a day for day basis. What checks are made on petrol sales and how are shifts arranged?
6. Sketch a layout of the station indicating distances between pumps and lanes and state why this layout was chosen.
7. Name ten accessories sold at this forecourt and state which items have the most rapid turnover.

Questions

1. Assume petrol sales have slumped in your garage.
   (a) Give possible reasons for this.
   (b) List possible ideas to attract custom. (I.M.I.)
2. 'Self-service' petrol stations have become a reality. Explain, with the aid of a sketch, how a self service petrol station is arranged and list the advantages of such a station over a conventional petrol station. (I.M.I.)
3. Detail the costs of running a petrol station and explain in detail how petrol costs can be controlled. (I.M.I.)
4. The Petroleum (Regulations) Acts closely govern the dispensing of petrol. Name 6 important parts of the regulations and state how you would ensure each of these was carried out. (I.M.I.)
5. List the basic knowledge which every forecourt attendant needs to know and state how you would ensure he was efficient at his job. (I.M.I.)
6. Cash and Credit are part of Petrol Sales. Explain how you would control each of these arrangements. (I.M.I.)
7. Name four important legal acts which govern the sales on a petrol forecourt. Briefly describe how each act can affect the forecourt and how you would ensure you were operating within the law in each case. (I.M.I.)
8. Self-service petrol stations have become popular. State and briefly describe 3 methods used to dispense petrol this way. (I.M.I.)
9. A high turnover of forecourt attendants is still prevalent to-day. Suggest reasons for this and how this problem can be overcome. (I.M.I.)
10. Detail the day to day running of a petrol station operating on the self-service principle. State the number of staff you would expect to employ and how petrol costs would be controlled. (I.M.I.)

List of Institutes and Associations

Institute of the Motor Industry (Inc.),
'Fanshaws',
Brickenden, HERTS.

A professional institute with various grades of membership which are usually obtained by examination and other requirements. The aim of the institute is to raise and maintain the status of the motor industry as a whole.

Institute of Road Transport Engineers,
1 Cromwell Place,
London, S.W.7.

A professional institute with various grades of membership which are usually obtained by examination and other requirements. The aim of the institute is to raise and maintain the status of the transport engineer and the transport industry.

Road Transport Industry Training Board,
Capitol House,
Empire Way,
Wembley, MIDDLESEX.

A government body which imposes a levy on all transport and garage organizations. The size of the levy depends upon the number of employees. Grants are payable to firms who operate satisfactory training programmes. On request, the R.T.I.T.B. will supply data concerning all aspects of training.

City and Guilds of London Institute,
76 Portland Place,
London, WIN 4AA.

An independent institute which offers certificates which can be obtained by examination passes. The C.G.L.I. is recognized throughout the world.

National Economic Development Office,
Millbank Tower,
21–41 Millbank.
London, S.W.1.

A government office which can supply on request, many valuable booklets dealing with motor vehicle distribution and repair.

Motor Agents Association,
201 Great Portland Street,
London, W.1.

This is an association of garage employers and represents them on various committees such as wage negotiation. Employers can use the M.A.A. for legal and other advice.

Garage Equipment Association,
11 Ironmonger Lane,
London, E.C.2.

This is a body which represents manufacturers, distributors and other people concerned with garage equipment. Advice on equipment and garage layout is given to members.

Society of Motor Manufacturers and Traders,
Farbes House,
Halkin Street,
London, S.W.1.

A society which has members drawn from manufacturers of vehicles, components, accessories and allied trades. The society represents the interests of its members by formulating economic and other policies associated with the motor industry. The Earls Court Motor Show is organized by this body.

Vehicle Builders and Repairers Association,
13–14 Park Place,
Leeds.

Membership of this association is open to all vehicle body builders and repairers whose premises and standards comply with those laid down by the Association.

Motor Industry Research Association,
Lindley,
Nr. Nuneaton,
Warwickshire.

All manufacturers of vehicles can obtain membership and obtain advice in connection with vehicle performance. Research into all problems connected with transport are conducted at the proving ground.

Her Majestys Stationery Office,
P.O. Box 569,
London, S.E.1.

All legal publications and other government journals are obtainable through this office or through a local stationery office which can be found in big cities. The Factories Act and similar controlling documents can be obtained from H.M.S.O. Prices of such documents are available upon request.

British Standards Institution,
2 Park Lane,
London, W.1.

Manufacturers and other interested parties form committees to set standards for all kinds of work. Copies of such standards can be obtained from the institution. A price list is available upon request.

Institute of Mechanical Engineers,
1 Birdcage Walk,
London, S.W.1.

A profession institute which has an Autombbile Division. Membership is available upon passing appropriate sections of the Institute's examinations along with other requirements.

Appendix II
C.G.L.I. Courses

Many changes have occurred in course numbers in recent years. To avoid confusion the 1972 course numbers are given in the text. To enable readers to compare the old courses and old course numbers with current courses and new numbers the following list has been compiled.

Course	Old number	New number
Motor Vehicle Technician	170	390
Motor Vehicle Mechanic	168	375
Motor Vehicle Electrician	169	375
Motor Vehicle Parts Department Practice	384	376
Motor Vehicle Craft Studies Part I	550	380
Light and Heavy Vehicle Mechanic Craft Studies Part II	551	381
Motor Vehicle Electricians Craft Studies Part II	552	381
Light Vehicle Partsmen's Craft Studies Part II	554	381
Vehicle Salesmanship	555	382
Vehicle Body Craft Studies (Parts II and III)	545,549	385
Vehicle Body Engineering Technician	318	395
Compression Ignition Engine Mechanics	447	379
Panel Beating	295	377
Vehicle Body Building	294	
Vehicle Painting and Industrial Finishing	296	387
Vehicle Body Trimming	297	
Vehicle Body Work	298	
Motor Vehicle Craft Studies Part III	559	381

NOTE: Some courses now overlap and will ultimately be phased out. For example the old 168 (375) will be replaced by 381 courses, 384 (376) will be replaced by 381. No fixed date has been agreed for the final phasing out of any course. The list will be useful for future reference by employers, training officers and other personnel concerned with training and education in service stations.

Road Haulage Association, 22 Upper Woburn Place, London, W.C.1.	An employers' association which has information to deal with all problems affecting road transport organizations.

There are many other associations which represent the public and motor industry as a whole. Some of these are the Automobile Association, Royal Automobile Club, Institute of Advanced Motorists, Motor Schools Association, British Motor Trade Association, Tyre Manufacturers' Conference Limited, National Tyre Distributors' Association Retread Manufacturers Association, The Motor and Cycle Trades Benevolent Fund.

Trade journals

Keeping up to date with equipment and techniques is possible by studying trade journals. There are a large number but the most popular are the *Motor Trader*, *The Service Station*, *The Garage and Motor Agent*, *Motor Transport*, *Garage and Transport Equipment* and *The Motor Industry*. Journals are issued by the various associations listed and two well known weekly magazines are *The Motor* and *The Autocar*. *Engineering, Materials and Design* is a monthly magazine.

A student would do well to peruse all the journals listed and decide which journal is essential for him. To keep abreast of new techniques in management and administration a particular journal can be selected which is relevant to the work he is doing.

INDEX